RESEARCHING
PERSONS
WITH MENTAL
ILLNESS

Applied Social Research Methods Series
Volume 30

APPLIED SOCIAL RESEARCH
METHODS SERIES

Series Editors:
LEONARD BICKMAN, Peabody College, Vanderbilt University, Nashville
DEBRA J. ROG, Vanderbilt University, Washington, DC

RESEARCHING PERSONS WITH MENTAL ILLNESS

Rosalind J. Dworkin

Applied Social Research Methods Series
Volume 30

SAGE Publications
International Educational and Professional Publisher
Newbury Park   London   New Delhi

For information address:

SAGE Publications, Inc.
2455 Teller Road
Newbury Park, California 91320

SAGE Publications Ltd.
6 Bonhill Street
London EC2A 4PU
United Kingdom

SAGE Publications India Pvt. Ltd.
M-32 Market
Greater Kailash I
New Delhi 110048 India

Printed in the United States of America

Library of Congress Cataloging-in-Publication Data

Dworkin, Rosalind J.
  Researching persons with mental illness / Rosalind J. Dworkin.
     p.   cm. — (Applied social research methods series; v. 30)
  Includes bibliographical references and index.
  ISBN 0-8039-3603-6 (cl). — ISBN 0-8039-3604-4 (pb)
  1. Mentally ill — Research — Methodology. I. Title. II. Series.
  (DNLM: 1. Data Collection — methods. 2. Mental Disorders.
3. Research Design. WM 20 D993r)
  RC337.D86 1992
  616.89'0072 — dc20

92-11719
CIP

92 93 94 95 96 10 9 8 7 6 5 4 3 2 1

Sage Production Editor: Judith L. Hunter

Contents

Acknowledgments

A book of this type cannot be written without the assistance and cooperation of a large number of people. First, I thank the two directors of the Community and Social Psychiatry Programs of Baylor College of Medicine, Dr. Comstock and Dr. Adams; they provided encouragement and resources for my research over the years. I also thank the administration and treatment staff of the Mental Health/Mental Retardation Authority of Harris County who, between 1983 and 1989, generously cooperated with me and my research teams.

Many thanks also go to Ruth L. Telschow, M.A., who assisted me by doing literature searches, analyzing data, and reading early versions of the manuscript. Margaret LeCompte, Ph.D., and Howard B. Kaplan, Ph.D., also have my thanks for their helpful suggestions. I also thank the many clinicians who worked with me on several projects that provided examples included in the text: John F. Aruffo, M.D.; Shaista Chunawala, M.D.; John H. Coverdale, M.D.; Lois C. Friedman, Ph.D.; Kim D. Grant, Ph.D.; H. Steven Moffic, M.D.; and Vicki Sloan, Ph.D. Patricia Gomez Carrion, M.D., and Lois C. Friedman, Ph.D., also have my gratitude for reading early versions of the manuscript. Their clinical expertise was extremely valuable, and their collegiality renewed my enthusiasm for multidisciplinary teamwork. I also wish to acknowledge the series editors, Leonard Bickman, Ph.D., and Debra Rog, Ph.D., and two anonymous reviewers for their suggestions. Finally, a very special thanks goes to my husband, Anthony Gary Dworkin, Ph.D., who provided years of professional advice and personal support.

Rosalind J. Dworkin, Ph.D.
October 1990

to Gary

1

Who Are the Mentally Ill?

A young woman wandered the hospital emergency room, testing each bed while alternately laughing and whimpering. A psychiatric technician asked her name, provoking a marked startle response.

After hearing detailed instructions, a middle-aged patient sat in her caseworker's office, rocking and holding the informed consent in her hand for nearly 10 minutes. When asked if she had signed the form, she cried and said that she didn't know what she was supposed to do with it.

He was an articulate, attractive young man who spoke about himself with quiet assurance. It was near the end of his presentation that he blamed himself for the 1985 Mexico City earthquake. He explained to his startled audience that he had not been there to concentrate on holding the world together.

All of the persons briefly described above were observed while under treatment for serious mental illness; they were also potential candidates as subjects in behavioral science research. Can they be interviewed? Can they complete a self-administered questionnaire? What reliability can be expected in their responses? What about the ethics of informed consent? These are some of the issues that must be confronted when researching persons with mental illness.[1]

Who are the mentally ill? The very question predisposes one to answer in generalities and stereotypes that assume a group homogeneity, which, upon closer inspection, does not exist. Although some people with mental illness may fit common stereotypes of being dangerous and unpredictable, some do not. Some will be found in mental hospitals; others seldom leave their own homes; and still others are employed in full-time jobs in their communities. The seriously mentally ill population is as varied as any other group of individuals. Nevertheless, the mentally ill are often seen as persons apart: definable and identifiable. They are an aggregate of people who consume considerable economic resources; about whom there are strong attitudes and sometimes fears; who have special institutions created for processing them; who are alternately medicalized and criminalized. Indeed, they represent subjects for a broad spectrum of research topics involving mental illness.

THE PREVALENCE OF MENTAL ILLNESS

Over the years, there have been many attempts at estimating the number of mentally ill persons in the population of the United States and elsewhere. Barrett and Rose (1986) and Weissman, Myers, and Ross (1986a) have edited volumes that summarize many of those studies. Some early epidemiological studies are of sufficient general interest that they are known to social scientists who are not specialists in the area. The Social Class and Mental Illness Study (Hollingshead & Redlich, 1958) and the Midtown Manhattan Study (Srole, Langner, Michael, Opler, & Rennie, 1962) are two such examples.

The Epidemiological Catchment Area Program (ECA), funded by the National Institutes of Mental Health (NIMH), is the most recent of the major epidemiological studies (Regier, Myers, Kramer, Robins, Blazer, Hough, Eaton, & Locke, 1984). Unprecedented in scope, with a sample of more than 18,000 adults (Weissman, Leaf, Tischler, Blazer, Karno, Bruce, & Florio, 1988), it focuses upon specific diagnosable pathology in the general populations of four predominantly urban areas and one rural state in the United States. Although the data have not been fully analyzed as yet, the program has yielded rates of specific psychiatric disorders independent of any prior case identification. Preliminary findings based upon the first three sites place the rate of major depression, one type of serious mental illness, between 2.2% and 3.5% of the population, and the rate of schizophrenia/schizophreniform disorders between 1.1% and 1.3% (Myers, Weissman, Tischler, Holzer, Leaf, Orvaschel, Anthony, Boyd, Burke, Kramer, & Stolzman, 1984). Over a lifetime, it is estimated that approximately 25% of the population will experience some type of psychiatric disorder (Myers et al., 1984). This certainly represents a significant number of individuals who have attributes that may evoke special societal responses, utilize special resources, require unique institutions to serve them, make an economic impact, and sometimes inspire political action. All of these attributes make the mentally ill an appropriate and salient group to research.

MENTAL ILLNESS IN SPECIAL POPULATIONS

This book is addressed especially to the social or behavioral scientist conducting research on seriously mentally ill persons. However, it must be noted at the beginning that one may be doing research on mentally ill people without intentionally designing a study on that population. In addition to the study of mental illness qua mental illness, there are many areas of research that necessarily must include recognition of mental pathology as an issue that potentially will have methodological impact. Especially within the realm of social problems and deviance, the mentally ill may overlap with other study populations. Such other populations include: criminals, homeless persons, substance abusers, the elderly, children, and AIDS patients.

Criminal Justice Population

With the popular media exploiting incidents of violence committed by persons said to be mentally ill, the researcher in deviance and criminology may come to expect to find large numbers within the criminal justice system who have psychiatric disorders. Contrarily, although psychiatrists are manifestly concerned with the association between violence and psychopathology (Krakowski, Volavka, & Brizer, 1986; Rappeport, Lassen, & Hay, 1967), they tend to de-emphasize to nonclinicians the numbers of psychiatric patients who are criminally involved.

Actually, there is wide variation in estimates of the proportion of criminal populations who are also mentally ill. Studies tend to be done in either jails or prisons, since these are identifiable, albeit biased, samples of the criminal population. Rates of severe mental illness in prison populations tend to be lower than in the general population according to Teplin (1990) because prior to imprisonment, seriously disturbed individuals are diverted to special forensic psychiatry prison units. Thus, prison samples are less likely to include inmates suffering from psychoses or serious organic syndromes unless the sample includes forensic units for the mentally disturbed.

However, researchers using samples drawn from jails are more likely to encounter inmates with mental illness because sorting of prisoners is generally not done in the temporary settings. Teplin gathered data comparable to that collected by the ECA Program and found that, after controlling for demographic differences, the prevalence of serious mental illness was two to three times higher within the jailed sample than among the general population.

The Urban Homeless

Research has described the population of homeless people as being disproportionally composed of mentally ill persons. In fact, the proportion of homeless said to be mentally ill has been estimated to be between 15% (Snow, Baker, Anderson, & Martin, 1986) and 90% (Bassuk, 1984), depending upon the methodology used to make the estimate. More recently, a review, sponsored by NIMH, of 10 studies estimated that the proportion of homeless people to be suffering from severe and persistent mental illness is approximately 30% (Tessler & Dennis, 1989). Thus researchers intending to study the homeless population must realize the potential of including mentally ill persons as part of any drawn sample and be cognizant of the methodological issues that may be raised.

Substance Abusers

There is mounting evidence that a large proportion of substance abusers have concurrent psychiatric disorders. Mulligan, Steer, and Fine (1978) found that among persons arrested for driving while intoxicated, 59% had MMPI profiles consistent with neurotic or psychotic patients. Similarly, Bell, Kelly, Clements, Warheit, and Holzer (1976) found that patients hospitalized for alcohol detoxification had significantly higher psychiatric disorder scores than those found in a survey of a general community population. More recently, H. Ross, Glaser, and Germanson (1988) found that among a population in treatment for substance abuse, two-thirds had current diagnoses of psychopathology, including 20% with major depression and 4.3% with a schizophrenic disorder.[2] Furthermore, one may expect to find substance abusers with mental illness caused by organic changes to the brain induced by prolonged use of one or more of these psychoactive substances. Overall, the ECA study found that psychiatric disorders and substance abuse co-occur more frequently than would be expected by chance (Lehman, Myers, & Corty, 1989). In short, when one does research on substance abusers, one must anticipate a higher proportion of mentally ill respondents than would be expected in a sample of the general population.

Elderly Populations

The proportion of the elderly with mental illness varies widely with the sampling method. Community samples yield rates of mental illnesses among the elderly that vary between 10% and 20% (Felton, 1982). Estimated rates of psychoses range between 4% and 8% (Felton) among general populations of the elderly. These rates are not dissimilar from the prevalence of illness found in adult populations. However, among those institutionalized in nursing homes, far higher rates of mental illness are estimated. In such populations, dementia[3] is disproportionally represented. Whereas the prevalence of dementia may be as high as 5% of the elderly living in the community (Gurland & Cross, 1982), at least one-third of nursing home residents may have dementia, and two-thirds of elderly patients admitted to longer-term psychiatric facilities have a diagnosis of dementia (Gurland, Mann, Cross, DeFeguerido, Shannon, Mann, Jenkins, Bennett, & Wilder, 1979). The most frequent types of dementia are of the Alzheimer's type and multi-infarct dementia.[4] Nevertheless, as many as 15% may have a reversible dementia secondary to other medical disorders (Gurland & Cross, 1982).

Children and Adolescents

A researcher who is studying children and adolescents may also encounter a significant subsample that meets the criteria for mental illness. The study of mental illness among children is an important and rapidly growing field. Unfortunately, there is presently in the United States no epidemiological study for children that is comparable to the ECA study for adults. However, Pliszka (1990) argues that the prevalence of childhood illness in the United States probably matches the 17.6% found for preadolescents in New Zealand by Anderson, Williams, McGee, and Silva (1987).

Some illnesses are specifically identified as childhood disorders, such as autism, attention deficit disorders, and conduct disorders. The latter is an example of what some have termed the "medicalization" of children's behavior problems. That is, defining and treating certain behaviors as symptomatic of illness in children that would not be treated if found in adults (Robins, 1983). Other disorders identified in the younger population may be adult disorders having an early onset. In particular, the ECA study identified four major adult disorders that commonly begin in late adolescence: anxiety disorder, major depression, drug abuse or dependence, and alcohol abuse or dependence (Christie, Burke, Regier, Raie, Boyd, & Locke, 1988).

AIDS or HIV Positive Populations

Finally, those social science researchers studying the current AIDS epidemic may encounter significant numbers of subjects who experience mental disorders. These disorders tend to be of two general types. First, AIDS patients sometimes develop psychological symptoms secondary to the AIDS diagnosis that are not unlike symptoms experienced by those with other terminal illness, such as cancer. Such symptoms may include anxiety, panic attacks, major depression, and suicidal ideations (Dilley, Ochitill, Perl, & Volberding, 1985; Faulstich, 1987; Perry & Markowitz, 1986).

More fundamental are mental disorders involving organic changes in either the brain or the central nervous system that are directly due to the HIV infection itself (S. Weiss & Biggar, 1986). One estimate suggests that between 50% and 70% of AIDS patients develop a clinically significant AIDS Related Dementia (ARD) (McArthur, 1987). Although such dementias usually accompany other AIDS symptoms, cases have been reported where that is the sole presentation (Navia & Price, 1987). Symptoms vary from mild apathy and withdrawal to more serious learning and memory difficulties, deteriorated cognitive functioning, hallucinations, and delirium (McArthur, 1987; Perry & Markowitz, 1986).

Researchers involved in any of these populations (to name only a few) will necessarily be involved with some proportion of subjects having a mental illness. Those researchers, like the researcher deliberately intending to study people with mental illness, will either have to confront issues of researching the mentally ill or risk using inappropriate theories and/or methodologies.

THE NATIONAL AGENDA IN
MENTAL ILLNESS RESEARCH

Over the past several years, there has been a profound change in emphasis in the field of mental health research led by NIMH. There has been a shift from overriding concern with the social bases of mental health to concern about the seriously mentally ill. This shift is best typified by the refocus of NIMH to a medical model. In 1985 NIMH was restructured to highlight the basic sciences (i.e., the neurosciences, the behavioral sciences, and the psychobiological sciences) and the major clinical disorders (Frazier, 1985). Then in 1986 NIMH designated as its foremost research priority the study of schizophrenia, the most complex and serious of the major mental illnesses (Keith & Matthews, 1988). A reinforcement of this changing focus was made when the 1990s were declared the Decade of the Brain (National Advisory Mental Health Council, 1989), with emphasis upon basic neuroscience research.

This represents a significant departure from an earlier public health model, which placed strong priority upon the prevention of illness by the improvement of the general population's mental health through community programs (Grob, 1987). When NIMH was formally established in 1949 (Grob), it strongly supported research efforts directed at models of social stress and its concomitants in a general population. Although much research was also supported in the etiology and treatment of disorder, there was a very heavy emphasis upon social components (Grob). Indeed, the very name, National Institutes of Mental *Health* suggested a focus upon nonclinical populations.

Today the social science contribution to the NIMH agenda may be focused most in service delivery research. Simultaneously, stress research, typically the domain of social scientists, has been subject to criticism. For example, Keith, Sirovatka, Matthews, and Corbett (1987, p. 4) comment, "the role of psychological or environmental stressors was being studied too often in isolation and not well integrated with a comprehensive biopsychosocial medical model." Scientific, social, and political factors have probably contributed to this shift. Research on biological processes has become possible with advances in genetics and neurobiology enabling investigations into diagnostic markers, brain chemistry, and brain functioning. The effectiveness of antipsychotic medications suggests the potential power of the biological approach. Furthermore, the deinstitutionalization movement, whereby large numbers of patients were discharged from state mental hospitals and urged to obtain treatment in their community, has made more visible the numbers and needs of the seriously mentally ill (Brown, 1985). There is increasing public attention on such urban problems as homelessness and substance abuse: phenomena that represent populations overlapping with the population of the mentally ill. The findings of the ECA programs have highlighted the magnitude of mental illness rates in the United States. This new epidemiologic data may be expected to have profound impact upon priorities within the mental health field, both in services and in research.

THE PURPOSE OF THE BOOK

In the vast amount of research done in the area of mental health, standard social science methodologies are used with great success. Personal interviews, large-sample surveys, self-administered questionnaires, and telephone random digit dialing supply quality data to test a range of hypotheses concerning stressors, social support, service utilization, and problems in living. However, researching the mentally ill brings with it unique issues both theoretical and methodological. One cannot merely transport existing methods and instruments tested on general populations to the mentally ill and expect that they will be appropriate with this special population. Chapter 2 will explore how theories of human behavior, which have been developed for general populations, may have limited applicability in a population whose defining characteristic is a label of mental pathology. Chapter 3 will elaborate upon how mental illness and its symptoms are defined and measured. Special problems in methodological design will be discussed in Chapter 4. Chapter 5 will discuss problems associated with direct data collection from persons with mental illness, especially how illness symptoms may introduce unanticipated problems, including ethical ones. Chapter 6 will discuss alternative data sources such as clinical charts, institutional data, and data banks. Finally, Chapter 7 will explore issues of research in multidisciplinary settings: mastering specialized vocabularies; gaining access to special locations; and collaborating with people from many different professions and research orientations.

The focus of the book will be upon the study of mentally ill adults at the individual level of analysis. It is aimed at social scientists, especially sociologists, who may have had little previous experience with this population. The purpose of this book is to alert researchers to special problems in researching the mentally ill; to provide some preparation for planning and implementing research in the area; and to offer suggestions for dealing with some unusual methodological issues.

NOTES

1. Mental illness is any clinically significant pattern of emotional or mental distress or disability (American Psychiatric Association, 1987). A fuller discussion of the definition of mental illness is presented in Chapter 3.

2. Schizophrenia is a group of severe psychotic disorders characterized by withdrawal from reality, delusions, hallucinations, inappropriate affect, and bizarre behavior *(Dorland's Medical Dictionary,* 1980).

3. Dementia is an organic loss of intellectual function *(Dorland's Medical Dictionary,* 1980).

4. Multi-infarct dementia is a loss of intellectual function caused by the cumulative effects of vascular disorder in the brain.

2

Applying Theory to the Study of Mentally Ill Persons

Any good research, be it basic or applied, on general populations or clinical ones, should derive from some theoretical perspective that guides the choice of variables and impacts design. The researcher has the option of selecting or creating theories specifically generated to explain or predict some aspect of mental illness phenomena. Where such theories are not available, one has the option of applying theories of physical disease and illness to mental illness, or converting clinical theories into empirically testable hypotheses, or borrowing theories developed in another arena of social science, the most common being theories of deviance and theories of the self.

Each option has its problems. Although there are many theories of etiology and treatment to be found in psychiatry and clinical psychology, they tend to be normative theories (i.e., conceptual frameworks suggesting how one ought to behave or what practices ought to be done), rather than empirical theories, as they are usually defined by researchers (i.e., sets of propositions that suggest explanatory relationships for some aspect of the observable world and are subject to verification). However, theories borrowed from other substantive areas carry with them assumptions that may be inappropriate for the study of mentally ill persons.

This chapter will be devoted to a discussion of some theories currently available for research on the mentally ill. Selected empirical theories will be examined that focus upon three types of phenomena: the etiology of mental illness, patient behavior models, and the contexts of treatment. The intent is not to provide an exhaustive review of available models; rather, a few representative perspectives will be examined for their utility and for the problems associated with their translation and application to researching mental illness.

ETIOLOGICAL THEORIES

One task of a theory is to explain the cause(s) or etiology of mental illness. There is little consensus among either mental health professionals or researchers with regard to which causal paradigms are most appropriate, or even how the multiple paradigms should be categorized. Three general models will be discussed here: the medical, the psychological, and the sociological.

Medical Models

Regardless of the particular method for classifying the theories, one family of models clearly consists of various biological or medical theories. These models, currently in the ascendancy among much of the psychiatric community, conceptualize mental illness as a disease of the brain that can be treated biologically, given the development of the proper medical technology.

For many years, biological etiologies have been assumed for the Organic Mental Syndromes and Disorders, such as senility, psychiatric symptoms caused by physical insult to the brain, or instances where gross physiological abnormalities can be observed in brain structure. However, the biological model is broadening to include many "functional" illnesses. Studies of brain structure and function, though facilitated by advances in medical technology that allow measurement and visual imaging heretofore unavailable, are still in their infancy and have produced mixed evidence of biological abnormality in the brains of patients with various diagnoses of mental illness (Martin & Preskorn, 1986).

Another line of biological inquiry focuses on the biochemistry of the brain and is exemplified by the hypothesis that the imbalance of the neurotransmitter, dopamine, in the brain accounts for the development of schizophrenic symptoms (Barchas, King, & Berger, 1984). Similarly, there are theories that major depression is due to abnormalities in norepinephrine and/or serotonin, which are other neurotransmitters (Winokur, 1986). Yet another neurotransmitter, GABA, may be implicated in anxiety, according to some recent research (Paul, 1988).

Other medical modelers are pushing back the boundaries of the etiology question. Encouraged by studies of families, and particularly of twins, geneticists are searching for specific hereditary factor(s). Bipolar illness (Clayton, 1986) and schizophrenia (Tsuang & Loyd, 1986) are two foci of genetic studies. So far, however, there has been no definitive link made between one of these illness and a specific chromosome location (Clayton, 1986).

Although the social scientist probably would not use these theories directly to develop models of the psychosocial aspects of mental illness, one may become involved in studies in which the biological interplays with other factors. Indeed, the biopsychosocial model implies that the biological, the psychological, and the social are all expected to be implicated in the etiology of mental illness as well as in its treatment. Thus it is important for the social scientist researching the mentally ill to become familiar with the biological theories. Standard textbooks such as Kaplan and Sadock (1989), Goldman (1988), and Winokur and Clayton (1986) can be helpful resources to the social scientist who needs more detailed information.

Psychological Models

Another etiological approach assumes that mental illnesses are functional and can be explained by psychology rather than physiology, by mind rather than brain phenomena. This approach encompasses many psychological, behavioral, and psychoanalytical approaches. Although these models are derived from diverse traditions, they are similar in tracing cause to emotional difficulties resulting from childhood events (Mechanic, 1969); that due to childhood trauma or inadequate early development, ego defenses are adopted that are manifested in psychopathology. The goal of treatment (e.g., psychoanalysis) is the resolution of these conflicts through symbolic reconstruction of one's life to build healthier defenses.

The best known of these theories are the explanations within the psychoanalytic paradigm represented by such work as that of Sigmund Freud and Adolf Meyer. Although there are important differences between the psychoanalytic theories, each begins by proposing that events occurring during childhood lay the foundations for mental health or illness. While Meyer emphasized how real (i.e., objectively observable) events shape personality, Freud focused upon the internal world of the individual's unconscious processes (Bowlby, 1988).

Few today would contend that childhood events are the direct and sole cause of serious psychotic illnesses. However, the pattern and nature of childhood attachments are considered by some to be important factors contributing to vulnerability to stress (Bowlby, 1988). Furthermore, these life experiences in their impact upon psychological functioning may indirectly cause psychiatric disorder (Rutter, 1986). In particular, a relationship between early parental loss and adult depression has been posited by many (see reviews by Bowlby, 1988; Gottschalk, 1990).

Theories more specific to the etiology of serious mental illness are exemplified by those that place the etiology of schizophrenia upon the double bind (Bateson, Jackson, Haley, & Weakland, 1956), and the schizophrenigenic family (Lidtz, 1963). These two theories, which are no longer considered credible, point to abnormalities within the family that lead to intrapsychic conflicts manifested in psychotic behavior during adulthood.

Psychological models have been extremely influential clinically, and the psychoanalytic paradigm particularly illustrates clinical orientations that are ill suited for empirical research. These theories generally were derived from unsystematic observations by clinicians of ill people only. They tend to yield hypotheses that are not empirically testable because they are not falsifiable. Although Freud is said to have considered psychoanalysis a scientific methodology, this theoretical paradigm has resisted research, perhaps due to the supposition that psychodynamically motivated behavior is extremely individualistic and not subject to generalizing statements. Furthermore, concepts in this tradition are especially difficult to operationalize. Transference, regression, repression, and trauma are difficult to measure independently of the outcome variable of interest.

Despite its clinical influence, past empirical evidence tended not to support the psychoanalytic models (Cockerham, 1989). Studies that have compared ill and non-ill people do not find the differences predicted by the psychodynamic approach (McGlashan, 1989). However, with the strengthening of the biomedical model, there is an effort on the part of the psychologically oriented to reconcile the two traditions and seek areas of compatibility (e.g. Bowlby, 1988; Gottschalk, 1990).

Sociological Models

The third family of etiological theories is more sociological and focuses upon the environment external to the individual. These theories include stress models, social mobility models, and the social definition perspective.

Stress is an important component in many etiological models. For several physical illnesses, stress is seen as a contributing risk factor to disease (Antonovsky, 1979). For example, it is hypothesized that stress compromises the immune system, such that infection is likely if exposure occurs during periods of high stress for the individual.

Theories linking stress or stressful life events to emotional states are widely used among social scientists. However, unlike the application of stress as an intervening variable for physical disease, stress is popularly used as a direct causal factor of such emotional discomforts as mild anxiety or minor depression. The theory of stress as the cause of serious illness grew out of the experience of World War II (Grob, 1987), which suggested that even in the normal individual, severe environmental stress can cause such emotional distress that normal coping mechanisms are rendered inadequate, and the individual suffers a mental disorder.

Nevertheless, by the mid-1980s the accumulated evidence suggested that the nature and strength of the link between stress and the development of the major psychiatric disturbances is not well understood. It is unlikely that stress is the single causal factor of the onset of a serious mental illness. More likely, it may be implicated in the recurrence of specific symptom periods. Thus stress may be a trigger (Zubin, Magazine, & Steinhauer, 1983) to an episode, or a shaper of the characteristics of the episode, given an underlying vulnerability (Neuchterlien & Dawson, 1984).

However, Day (1986) warns against depending upon unsupported assumptions about the nature of everyday life and life changes experienced by an individual with a mental disorder. The customary life events scales, such as Holmes and Rahe's (1967), may not be generalizable to the lives of people with mental illness. Alternatively, relying upon the individual's subjective interpretation of events can introduce the danger of confusing the causal direction: Does an event perceived as a stressor precipitate a symptom exacerbation, or is an event defined as especially stressful because of an impending psychotic episode?

The inclusion of social support as a buffer against stress raises similar translation considerations. An objective measure of support introduces unwarranted assumptions about how the situation is perceived by the individual. A behavior may be intended as supportive, but may not be interpreted as such by someone mentally ill. Moreover, the question of the appropriate causal order is relevant here as well (Berkman, 1986). Furthermore, Berkman (1984) and Broadhead, Kaplan, James, Wagner, Schoenback, Grimson, Heyden, Tibblin, and Gehlbach (1983) cite the need to separate the concepts of social networks and social support. With the mentally ill, one should consider whether social networks are a source of stress, or a buffer against stress, or curvilinear in their relationship to stress depending upon the nature and/or severity of the illness.

On the macro level, Warner (1985), in a meta-analysis of the cross-cultural prevalence of schizophrenia, suggests that the stress of industrialized living and low socioeconomic status may increase the rates of this disorder. However, as Warner acknowledges, cross-cultural comparisons are extremely difficult to make, given variations in diagnostic criteria and instrumentation. Nevertheless, work such as Warner's can create a bridge between the stress theories and the second socio-environmental theory.

The second socio-environmental type of theory developed out of early findings that the rates of mental illness tend to be lower among the more privileged social groups and higher among the disadvantaged (Faris & Dunham, 1939; Hollingshead & Redlich, 1958; Srole et al., 1962). These findings are subject to two alternative causal explanations. The social selection hypothesis posits that mentally ill persons tend to "drift" down in socioeconomic status. The social causation hypothesis reverses the causal arrow, positing that the environment created by poverty is implicated in the etiology of mental illness. Day's (1986) theory of toxic environments suggests that chronic stress may be the connection between social class and mental illness. The work of Link, Dohrenwend, and Skiodol (1986) on stressful traits of initial occupations of people diagnosed with schizophrenia suggests that this may be a promising area for additional theoretical development.

The final theory of the etiology of mental illness to be discussed is a social definition or labeling theory, which has attracted much attention over the past 15 years. This is a sociologistic theory borrowed from the area of deviance and purported to be a complete theory of mental illness. In 1966 Thomas Scheff combined two scholarly ideas. The first was the stance of Thomas Szasz (1961) that mental illness does not exist as an objective reality. The second idea was Lemert's (1951) concepts of deviance and social labeling. In combining those two ideas, Scheff placed the phenomenon of mental illness completely outside the individual and into the social environment. His labeling theory proposed that mental illness is a social role with an identity and career pattern, and that societal reaction to an act of primary residual deviance is the most important determinant of entry into that role; that without the process of reaction and labeling, the deviant behavior would be transitory and there would be no attribution of mental illness.

Labeling theory had an immense impact upon sociologists studying the mentally ill, but began to lose its influence by 1980. As more empirical data were analyzed, and as social scientists began to accept contributions from other disciplines, the accrued evidence failed to support the basic propositions of labeling theory (Gove, 1982). Although it is no longer generally accepted as a complete theory of mental illness, its concepts of societal reaction and patient careers are still useful. Recent applications of labeling theory usually acknowledge an underlying mental pathology within the individual, and study the labeling process as it is superimposed over the illness and as that process interacts with symptoms to produce self-fulfilling prophecies and other effects.

The loss of labeling theory's primacy may have been due to the greater acceptance by social scientists of the existence of mental illness as something real within an individual. Historical changes impacted another basic assumption of the theory. Scheff saw the mental hospital as the primary socialization instrument for the acquisition of the mentally ill identity. With deinstitutionalization, treatment of the severely mentally ill is no longer principally located within hospital walls (Brown, 1985). Not only are hospital stays far shorter than they were 25 years ago, but treatment also varies considerably across states, with many of the "new chronic" patients never experiencing hospitalization (Bachrach, 1988). While this violates an important assumption of the labeling model, it also generates new hypotheses regarding the effects of varying treatment locales upon the roles and careers of mentally ill persons.

THEORIES OF PATIENT BEHAVIOR

Another major focus of theoretical development has been in the area of patient behavior. The concept of the sick role and the health belief model, both central in the social psychology of medicine, will be emphasized in this discussion as examples of difficulties that can be encountered when adopting theories of patient behavior to the study of mental illness.

The Sick Role

Central in many theories of patient behavior is Parson's (1951, 1975) idea of the sick role. Although subject to criticism and modification (West, 1989), it has been a heuristic tool for medical sociologists. However, sick-role models are considered by many to be inappropriately applied to the mentally ill (Cockerham, 1989), or to any illness that is chronic or that carries social stigma (Twaddle, 1979). Morgan, Calnan, and Manning (1985) observed that the mentally ill are often reluctant to accept sick roles. Indeed, denial of any illness or problem is frequently a characteristic encountered among mentally ill people.

There is some utility to the application of the sick role concept to the study of mental illness. A potential application of the concept could involve not the patients' adoption of the sick role, but the mechanisms and the effects of having the sick (or impaired) role attributed to the patient by others. For example, Denzin and Spitzer (1966) attempted to define the conditions under which mental hospital staff view patients as occupying sick roles. The sick role may be iatrogenic or may prevent patients from being seen as responsible for their behavior (Arluke, 1988). Likewise, the acceptance of a sick role may be situation specific. The sick role may be alternately accepted and shed depending upon the changing social environment.

Cognitive Theories of Behavior

An influential system of theories used by the behavioral sciences in medicine is composed of the various cognitive theories of behavior. These include the health belief model, the application of locus of control models to health behaviors, and behavioral intention theories. For a fuller description of each, see the reviews by Kirscht (1988), K. Wallston and Wallston (1982), and Ritter (1988), respectively. One could consider the models as distinct theoretical perspectives, as does Gochman (1988), or as potentially interconnected, as implied by DiMatteo and DiNicola (1982). Whether distinct or interconnected, they present similar problems to the researcher wishing to translate them for use in explaining the health behavior of mentally ill persons.

The health belief model was originally generated to predict preventive behaviors, such as seeking immunization, but has since been used in studies of a wider range of health behaviors, including compliance with treatment. The model, as delineated by Rosenstock (1966) and Becker (1974), specifies conditions under which individuals will seek and comply with health care regimens. These conditions include belief in one's susceptibility to illness and the severity of the disease; belief in the efficacy of the treatment; belief in one's self-efficacy; and perceptions of the relative costs of the treatment. The model has been modified in various ways to include locus of control concepts, (B. Wallston, Wallston, Kaplan, & Maides, 1976); cues to action (Becker & Maiman, 1975); and the systematic addition of social-normative factors (DiMatteo & DiNicola, 1982). The model has been used in mental health in a rather piecemeal manner, mainly to study medication compliance. Kelly, Mamon, and Scott's (1987) work is a recent example of an attempt to test the model more completely.

This theory serves as an excellent illustration of how theories about physical disease are translated with great difficulty into theories about mental disorder. The health belief model implicitly assumes that people adopt a logical means-end schema as a basis for their action (i.e., reasoned action). It also assumes that illness is negatively valued and that the individual is an autonomous actor.

Although a specific physical disease may challenge any one of these assumptions, mental illness challenges nearly all of them simultaneously, rendering the health belief model inappropriate without extensive modification and additions. People who exhibit symptoms of thought disorder, delusions, or dementia also may exhibit a weakening of means-end rationality. The mentally ill person also may evaluate the symptoms differently from the way others do. There may be denial of symptoms. Conversely, symptoms socially defined as indicative of disease, and thus negatively evaluated by others, may be positively valued by the person experiencing those symptoms (Estroff, 1981).

Finally, these theories assume actor volition; however, mentally ill persons often experience assaults on their autonomy. Internally, such assaults may be in the form of hallucinatory voices compelling the individual to particular behavior. Externally, autonomy may be compromised from several directions as others actively seek help for the patient's symptoms. Assaults upon autonomy may originate from familial, medical, and legal institutions empowered to commit an individual for involuntary treatment. It is these various pathways by which someone may come into treatment for a mental illness that must be taken into account when evoking theories such as the health belief model to account for service utilization. Moreover, patient functioning and patient interpretation of symptoms will specify conditions for the applicability of the theory. Furthermore, since symptomatic and symptom-free periods are interspersed over time, models of patient behavior must become correspondingly complex.

The model could, however, be expanded to include variables that may make it more adaptable to questions involving mental illness. For example, Mechanic (1969) suggested that such models should include psychological processes that could distort the actor's perception of reality. A fuller model would also include a measurement of those actor needs that may conflict with his or her assumption of the sick role, as well as the actor's alternative interpretations of symptoms, and variations in the tolerance levels of those in contact with the symptomatic individual. All of these additional variables strengthen the basic health belief model because they reduce the number of assumptions that must be made about the actor's definition of reality, and his or her autonomy.

CONTEXTS OF TREATMENT

Another area of theoretical development involves exploring the effects of the treatment context upon the behavior of persons with a mental illness. Stanton and Schwartz's (1954) early research suggested that the institutional milieu creates maladaptive behavior. The work on this topic most widely known is Goffman's (1961) theory of the mental hospital as a total institution. In this work, he described how prolonged institutionalization may produce deviant behaviors that are attempts to adapt to the total institution environment and are not in themselves symptomatic of illness.

Whether Goffman's work was an accurate description of the hospital experience at that time is a moot point. Of more current concern is the extent to which his findings are time-bound, and the extent to which the total institution concept represents a heuristic perspective today.

A formal theory is needed specifying the conditions under which institutional behavior is likely to occur. Testable hypotheses need to be generated, using quantifiable variables applied across many types of treatment facilities in either longitudinal or quasi-experimental designs that are carefully controlled. Researching the institutional syndrome is very difficult to do. Wing (1962) suggests that not only are length of time hospitalized and degree of postadmission stresses important variables, but that patient characteristics at the time of admission are also important to consider. Such characteristics would include intensity of symptoms and whether the hospitalization was an involuntary commitment or a voluntary one. Moreover, ward environments may vary in emotional tone, activities, and interpersonal interactions (Kellam, Schmelzer, & Berman, 1966; Mechanic, 1969; Stanton & Schwartz, 1954), and these too may be hypothesized to affect the degree of institutional syndrome.

Contemporary theories of the effects of treatment context upon the mentally ill must recognize the vast changes in the system of treatment that have occurred since Goffman's work in the early 1960s. Deinstitutionalization has occurred across the United States (Brown, 1985), thereby rendering much of Goffman's findings temporally ungeneralizable. Since only a small cadre of people remains institutionalized for a long period of time, one would expect some selection factor(s) to operate. Factoring in the natural course of illness is critical because the natural course of some illnesses is marked by increased social withdrawal, even among those not hospitalized. If the less withdrawn and apathetic are discharged earlier, a badly skewed hospitalized sample will confound any potential findings. Separating these selection effects from a true institutional syndrome poses both theoretical and methodological challenges. It requires an understanding of the expected course of various mental illnesses as well as an understanding of organizational processes. Finally, since much of the treatment of the seriously ill occurs not within the walls of the total institution but in an outpatient environment, a continuum of totality or restrictiveness of environment should be a component of any theory dealing with treatment context today.

THE BIOPSYCHOSOCIAL MODEL

Obviously, there are several theoretical orientations to the understanding of mental illness phenomenon. The biopsychosocial model is an effort to integrate rival paradigms in psychiatry. According to Engel (1977) there are biological, psychological, behavioral, and social components t psychiatric illness, as well as to illnesses that have traditionally been an accepted part of the biomedical model. The clinician must be cognizant of each of these components in order to understand the conditions under which the presence of physical defects become experienced as illness; the timing of the onset of illness; the timing of help seeking; and the efficacy of treatment. The biopsychosocial model can also be utilized as a very general approach to the study of mental illness in which biological, psychological, and social components are recognized as contributors to the studied phenomenon. The basic model has been adapted in various ways to generate multiple-causation theories of etiology of serious mental illness. A typical approach is the diathesis-stress interactive model (Liberman, Falloon, & Wallace, 1984), which posits that schizophrenic symptoms develop from social stressors and the inability to cope with them, interacting with a preexisting biologically derived vulnerability (i.e., the diathesis).

Although the model admits the importance of sociological concepts, the formulation has problems for the social scientist. It is an orientation, not really a theory. Furthermore, the social part of the model is limited to social psychological and cultural belief variables. Social structural and organizational factors are excluded. Armstrong (1987) argues that while appearing to accept the importance of social variables, the biopsychosocial model may merely be a way of neutralizing the independent efforts of social science; that Engel's model minimizes the essentially social nature of the definition and attribution of illness, maintaining the dominance of biomedicine.

Noticeable among most theories generated from the general biopsychosocial model is the inherent assumption that the process conforms to the same order as the word: that the biological is fundamental. The theories postulate that first activated is a biological vulnerability: a genetic predisposition, a birth trauma, or an imbalance of neurotransmitters. To this is added some psychological or developmental inadequacy. Then the symptoms are tripped by environmental stress. However, this order should be considered an empirical question rather than an assumption. The presumed causal direction is being directly challenged in the development of depression by Mirowsky and Ross (1989a, 1989b). They contend that the data showing an association among biochemical changes, stress, and depression are sufficiently ambiguous that the biochemical abnormalities could be an effect rather than a cause. They posit a model of depression in which social structurally induced strain creates perceptions of threat and powerlessness that affect mood and noradrenergic levels.

Indeed, the issue does remain open. Other permutations of the causal order could be hypothesized. Furthermore, the causal order may not be fixed, but may vary across types of illness. Teasing out the true processes under specified conditions will require the joint contributions of scientists from many disciplines, including the social sciences.

CONCLUSION

Various conceptual issues and assumptions must be explicitly dealt with as one adopts a theory and specifies models and/or hypotheses for researching the mentally ill. Below are a series of questions that could be considered.

Is a single or multiple causation model being proposed? Does the theory acknowledge other models of mental illness that have demonstrated validity? How do these models interact for an overall understanding of the phenomenon under study? Although single causation models are attractive because of their parsimony, eclectic models probably will ultimately have greater explanatory power.

What assumptions are being made regarding the nature of mental illness? Is one assuming an objective phenomenon, called mental illness, that exists beyond the subjective definition of social actors? What are the theoretical costs and profits of making or not making this assumption?

What assumptions are being made regarding the rationality of the population? Is the assumption of reasoned action justifiable? Is the assumption compatible with the theory's assumption about the existence of mental illness?

Does the theory rely upon the mentally ill's perceptions of a situation? What are the assumptions regarding the nature of those perceptions? What might be the impact upon the model of the perceptions of others? Will this affect the hypothesized causal direction? Does reliance upon the patient's perceptions address the questions being asked?

To what extent is the theory time- and/or culture-bound? Have conditions changed sufficiently that the theory, however heuristic, may have become obsolete? Can conditional variables make such a theory more generalizable across time?

Are assumptions being made about the causal direction that should be empirically determined? What special variables need to be included that are unique to the study of mental illness and are not included in general models? Possible intervening variables include: the level of functioning exhibited by subjects; the type and/or intensity of symptoms; the types and characteristics of medication prescribed and/or taken; and the diagnosis.

3

Diagnosis and Other Measurements of Illness

In this chapter the measurement of some basic psychiatric variables will be discussed. The major measurement, actually a categorical attribute, to be examined is diagnosis. Currently, diagnosis is a controversial topic: Its meaning and utility are being challenged both in research and in clinical schools of thought. Nevertheless, the researcher can ill afford to ignore diagnostic issues. There will be pressures within a multidisciplinary setting to incorporate diagnosis into a study regardless of the position the individual researcher takes. Thus, several issues of diagnosis will be considered in this chapter: its conceptual utility; classification schemata; inter-diagnostician reliability; instrumentation; and markers and gold standards. Following that, other approaches to the measurement of illness will be considered. However, first there must be some discussion of the relationship between measurement of mental illness and the identification of "caseness."

WHAT IS A CASE?

A fundamental issue in research on the mentally ill is the measurement of mental illness and the identification of people said to be cases of some type of mental illness. Unfortunately, according to Kendell (1986) there is no conceptual definition of mental illness or mental health that has the consensus of the psychiatric discipline. Likewise, there is no definition acceptable to all in the social sciences. Kendell suggests that four strategies might be used to define mental illness. First, one could make no attempt to define it, but leave the construct unexamined. This, he says, is the strategy adopted by the World Health Organization. The second strategy is to define the concept vaguely as anything that conforms to contemporary medical opinion. The revised *Diagnostic and Statistical Manual* (DSM-III-R) of the

American Psychiatric Association (1987) is purported to be using the second strategy. The editors of that very influential manual maintain that there is no definition that specifies precise boundaries. However, DSM-III-R defines *mental disorder* as any "clinically significant pattern . . . associated with present distress (a painful symptom) or disability (impairment in one or more important areas of functioning) or with a significantly increased risk of suffering death, pain, disability, or an important loss of freedom" (p. xxii). The third approach to defining mental illness is to provide an explicit definition with clear rules of application. Clearly, this is the preferred approach for research, but Kendell maintains it is a strategy that no one has (successfully) adopted in psychiatry. The fourth strategy is to define mental disorder as those problems for which psychiatrists are currently consulted. This is essentially a social definitional strategy, which Kendell favors as being the most realistic.

Psychiatrists generally follow DSM-III-R's medical model lead. Even though the editors of DSM-III-R accept the idea of a continuum of impairment, in actuality it is little used in the clinical setting. Rather, the essentially continuous concept of health/illness is converted into a dichotomous concept: caseness. Schwab and Schwab (1978, p. 42) defines *case* as "an instance of illness or injury." An implicit and often fluctuating cutting point marks where normal variation ends and aberration begins. The placement of the cutting point is socially, economically, and sometimes politically derived, changing across time and cultures. The cutting point, albeit arbitrary, separates the case from the noncase. This dichotomization reflects basic clinical decision making: to treat or not to treat (Klerman, 1989).

The concept of case is very early operationalized. Wing, Mann, Leff, and Nixon (1978) and Vaillant and Schnurr (1988) support the use of "case" as an operationalized variable and dismiss the necessity for a conceptual definition. "The case can be used in any way that clinicians and research workers wish, but if they wish to communicate with others, they will need to provide a usable definition" (Vaillant & Schnurr, 1988, p. 313).

Because there is no generic definition of mental illness (i.e., there is no universal agreement on the construct), individuals presenting similar symptoms may be variously diagnosed as mentally ill or not. Furthermore, caseness is greatly affected by the choice of cutting point. As a consequence, the application of cutting points to delineate caseness presents a dilemma. Too stringent a standard for defining a case over-identifies cases, while too lax a standard underidentifies. Epidemiologists conceptualize this issue of validity as a cross-classification, such as presented in Table 3.1.

Sensitivity refers to the percentage of cases correctly identified, or the rate of true positives [in Table 3.1: (A/A + C) × 100] (Lilienfeld & Lilienfeld, 1980). *Specificity* refers to the percentage of noncases correctly identified, or the rate of true negatives [(D/D + B) × 100] (Lilienfeld & Lilienfeld). The difficulty in applying the formulas is establishing the true presence of the referent phenomenon with the use of a gold standard. However, in the absence of absolute standards, the known groups method is used with its inherent problems: the selection of the proper groups; the avoidance of unknown confounding variables; and the problems of applicability to less extreme groups or situations than are ordinarily selected for the validity study. Thus, a measure of caseness may be sensitive and/or specific for identification of extremely ill inpatients, but could fail when applied to less severely ill persons.

For most clinicians and clinical researchers, *mental disorder* is defined operationally as whatever their diagnostic nosology (i.e., classification schema) says it is. Furthermore, diagnosis is the criterion for caseness: If an individual is a case, there is a diagnosis; if an individual is diagnosable, he or she is a case. More than the continuum of mental illness, it is the dichotomy of caseness that concerns so much of psychiatric research; case identification; risk factors of developing into a case; the behavior of cases; the treatment of cases; the outcome for cases. Thus it is important to understand the concept of diagnosis and the various diagnostic schemata used in research to identify and label cases.

CONCEPTUALIZING DIAGNOSIS

Diagnosis, or the determination of the nature of a case of illness, is considered by most medically oriented caregivers to be central to the treatment process. Diagnosis is both a process and a label. The diagnosis sometimes implies a cause, or etiology; it often implies a course of treatment, or alternative treatment strategies; and it usually implies a prognosis. Although it is a key clinical procedure, there have been controversies even among clinicians over the years as to the meaning, utility, and consequences of applying a diagnosis to an individual (Dumont, 1987; Freedman, Brotman, Silverman, & Hutson, 1986).

Table 3.1
Validity of a Test for Caseness:
Possible Outcomes

	The True Situation	
Test Result	Illness Present	Illness Absent
Positive	True Positive (Valid Measure) A	False Positive (Invalid Measure) B
Negative	False Negative (Invalid Measure) C	True Negative (Valid Measure) D

The many issues involved in diagnosis have implications for the researcher as well as for the clinician. Fundamentally, the researcher must decide if mental state is to be conceptualized as a continuum whereby one may speak of degrees of health or illness. A continuum implies that illness and health are ideal types, rather than actual states dependent upon some arbitrary cutting point. Alternatively, one may conceptualize illness and health as a dichotomy: One is either ill (a case) or not. If one is ill, symptoms may be more or less severe at any given time. Furthermore, illness is subdivided into specific diagnoses according to a selected nosology.

The continuum approach lends itself better to research needs because of the ease with which it can be handled statistically. Clinicians, however, use the dichotomy approach because it lends itself to the identification of cases to be treated. It is through diagnosis that the distinction is made between those with mild symptoms of discomfort that exist in the general population and those who are so seriously mentally ill that treatment is warranted. Clinicians will usually contend that the difference between the two groups is not only one of intensity, but one of kind.

Recently, Mirowsky and Ross (1989a) have argued that diagnosis has utility neither for the researcher nor for the clinician. They contend that diagnosis is a weak and unreliable measurement, which groups symptoms into categories that do not correspond to statistically valid factors, and that in so grouping, detail and sensitivity are lost. Counterarguments contend that the diagnostic process is becoming increasingly reliable; that diagnosis is necessary to the identification of caseness through which clinician involvement is justified (Klerman, 1989); and that there is recognition by some psychiatrists that there are continua underlying categorical diagnoses (Tweed & George, 1989).

In fact, the researcher often has little choice as to whether diagnosis is to be a variable. The reality is that as long as clinicians use diagnosis, the researcher will probably need to do so as well. In etiological studies it is the primary dependent variable. Service utilization studies will find that access to treatment and treatment priorities are often defined in terms of broad diagnostic groups. Investigations of caregivers will find that clinician perceptions, behaviors, and role expectations are impacted by diagnosis and the diagnostic process. Diagnosis is also meaningful to the researcher as an important screening variable by which samples or subsamples are defined. Sixty-three percent of the articles appearing in two major psychiatric journals use diagnosis as an inclusionary or exclusionary criterion (Reich, Black, & Jarjoua, 1987). Alternatively, diagnosis is used as a key descriptive variable of importance equal to the socio-demographic variables familiar to social scientists. Furthermore, for researchers to be able to link findings to applications in the psychiatric world, diagnosis is a basic variable if medical cooperation or acknowledgment is desired.

Nevertheless, the researcher needs to exercise caution when using diagnostic labeling. Preferably, diagnosis is used as a characteristic attributed to an individual, rather than as a trait defining the individual as an entity (Mirowsky & Ross, 1989a). Just as medical sociologists prefer the term *person with a disability* over *disabled person*, perhaps the psychiatric researcher should not refer to a respondent as a "schizophrenic," but as a "person who meets the diagnostic criteria for schizophrenia," or a "patient who is diagnosed with schizophrenia." Admittedly, this can be stylistically awkward when writing.

DIAGNOSTIC NOSOLOGIES

Diagnostic and Statistical Manuals of Mental Disorders

For decades, American psychiatry has been trying to codify mental disorders into a universally accepted nosology. The effort set its first milestone with the publication of the *Diagnostic and Statistical Manual of Mental Disorders* (DSM) published in 1952. Other editions have been released, with a revision of the third edition (DSM-III-R), published in 1987 (American Psychiatric Association, 1987), and a fourth edition in preparation.

The DSM series, although not universally accepted, is the classification schema commonly used by American psychiatrists during recent years. Use of the DSM schema is said to facilitate the diagnostic process and third party, or insurance, payment (Nelson, 1986; Silverman & Brotman, 1986), thereby accounting for some of its popularity. Also, DSM is often used by psychiatrists in other nations, and by other mental health professionals.

The modifications made with each revision vary considerably. Some of the alterations introduced with new editions have been changes in nomenclature. Major affective disorders (DSM-III) became mood disorders (DSM-III-R), a change that appears to necessitate only a simple translation of terms. Other changes involve the specification of additional detail that may alleviate some ambiguities. However, some changes may pose problems to the researcher. Allowing the co-occurrence of anxiety disorder with other diagnoses in DSM-III-R but not in DSM-III, or the elimination in DSM-III of schizophrenia, latent type, found in DSM-II are examples where conversion from one edition to another may present problems.

The *Diagnostic and Statistical Manual* proposes a multi-axial classification with each of five axes containing different information deemed clinically useful. Axis I contains the information regarding clinical syndromes, such as schizophrenia; Axis II includes the developmental and personality disorders, such as dependent personality disorder; Axis III describes physical diseases, such as rheumatoid arthritis, that are not necessarily implicated in the mental disorder but may be relevant to understanding or treating the patient; Axis IV notes acute and chronic psychosocial stressors arranged on a continuum from none to catastrophic; and Axis V rates the level of functioning, measured on a 90-point scale. The manual itself is almost entirely devoted to the specification of Axes I and II. In a volume of 516 pages (excluding the index) a mere 4 pages are devoted to Axes III, IV, and V.

Each diagnosis receives a unique five-digit code identifying the disorder and its subclassification. For example, 296.44 is the code given to "bipolar disorder, manic, with psychotic features." The numbering system is arbitrary and does not imply any quantitative meaning. In addition to illness codes, there are special codes for conditions that are treated by psychiatrists but are not considered to be mental disorders. Diagnoses are typically arranged in hierarchies and are described in terms of a set of inclusion-ary and exclusionary criteria, as well as differential diagnoses, and subtypes.

International Classification of Diseases

There are several alternatives to the DSM schemata. One that may be familiar to the medical researcher is the International Classification of Diseases (ICD), assembled and published by the World Health Organi-zation. ICD is currently revised every 10 years, and is now in its ninth edition. This schema, purporting to categorize all known medical dis-orders, includes a section on mental disorders. There is an adaptation of the ICD-9 titled *International Classification of Diseases, 9th Revi-sion, Clinical Modification* (ICD-9-CM), which is published by the U.S. Department of Health and Human Services (1980). The ICD-9-CM numbering system is compatible with and considerably overlaps the DSM-III schema, but is not as detailed in its subclassifications of mental disorders. Furthermore, the ICD-9-CM does not provide de-tailed inclusionary and exclusionary criteria for each diagnosis. Hence, two users could employ the same terminology, but with different mean-ings attached. However, since it is used internationally for reporting morbidity, the coding schema can be quite useful for the researcher.

Research Diagnostic Criteria
and Other Schemas

Developed under the auspices of NIMH, the Research Diagnostic Criteria or RDC (Endicott, Andreasen, & Spitzer, 1975) is another frequently used diagnostic schema. Unlike the DSM series, it was developed primarily for research use rather than for clinicians. The RDC was generated in 1975 to provide more detailed diagnostic criteria than was currently available in DSM-II. The RDC is not intended to be an exhaustive catalog of diagnoses, but is meant to provide careful diagnostic guidelines for screening patients for research protocols. The emphasis is on the researcher's ability to generate a subject pool that is diagnostically homogeneous.

In addition to the DSM series and the RDC, there are several lesser-used diagnostic schema such as the St. Louis criteria (Feighner, Robins, Guze, Woodruff, Winokur, & Munoz, 1972), and the Tsuang and Winokur (1974) criteria. However, these minor schema vary in comprehensiveness, with some being specific to the diagnosis of a very small selection of disorders. Unless there are specific reasons to do otherwise, the choice of either the RDC or the DSM-III-R schemata would be preferred. They are known to most potential readers of the empirical literature and would facilitate cross-study comparability.

Making the Choice

The choice among the schemata can have important consequences in a research study, as each will define a patient population somewhat differently, and in so doing will impact research design in significant ways. For example, the DSM-III-R and the Feighner criteria for schizophrenia include a 6-month criterion, making the onset of symptoms and the earliest date of the schizophrenia diagnosis a half-year apart. The RDC does not have that criterion. Hence, in conforming strictly to the DSM criteria, one could not sample schizophrenics at the time of diagnosis and assume that this marks the approximate onset of the illness, or even the beginning of treatment. To include individuals at the onset of schizophrenic symptoms, one would also have to include other DSM diagnoses, such as schizophreniform and atypical psychoses, which often, but not always, get converted to schizophrenia after 6 months.

Studies comparing various diagnostic schema (Berner, Katschnig, & Lenz, 1986; Stephens, Astrup, Carpenter, Shaffer, & Goldberg, 1982) in the details of their respective diagnostic criteria report wide variation in criteria for the major disorders. Applying 11 schemata to a sample of 200 admissions, Berner et al. (1986) found a fivefold difference between the broadest and the narrowest of the systems. Furthermore, not all who passed the narrowest criteria also passed the widest. In a study of the reliability of diagnoses of schizophrenia subtypes, Gruenberg, Kendler, and Tsuang (1985) found that concordance between nosological systems was highest between DSM-III and RDC ($\kappa = .93$).

Although each nosology has its own idiosyncrasies, there are problems general to nearly all the schemata that need to be considered when using any diagnostic system in research. Over time, specific behaviors have been alternately defined as a diagnosable disorder or not. For example, until 1973, homosexuality had been classified as a disorder, but was dropped in DSM-II. Conversely, DSM-III-R includes an appendix of "proposed diagnostic categories needing further study" (American Psychiatric Association, 1987, p. 365), which includes such classifications as sadistic personality disorder and the self-defeating personality disorder and late luteal phase dysphoric disorder (i.e., premenstrual stress syndrome). One could speculate that the dismissal of homosexuality (Silverman, 1986) and the proposal of the three new disorders might be as much a function of sociopolitical forces as it is a function of the state of the psychiatric discipline.

Within a classification schema, there may be considerable overlap of symptoms from one diagnosis to another. For example, in DSM-III-R, hallucinations are among the inclusionary criteria for 27 different diagnoses. Conversely, there are few instances in which there is a single necessary and sufficient defining symptom for a diagnosis. Usually, a patient must exhibit several symptoms on a long inclusionary list to satisfy the criteria for that diagnosis. Johnstone (1986) observes that, other than the presence of some psychotic feature that is shared with other diagnoses, there is no other single defining characteristic for the schizophrenia diagnosis. A person diagnosed with major depressive syndrome does not necessarily have to have a depressed mood; loss of interest in pleasure is an alternative criterion.

Thus, there can be considerable heterogeneity within any one diagnostic category. For example, even beyond the subtypes of schizophrenia (DSM-III-R has five: disorganized, catatonic, paranoid, residual, and undifferentiated), there is general recognition of additional dimensions of heterogeneity. There is current discussion of negative and positive symptom types of schizophrenia, which imply widely different behaviors and differential response to various therapies.

Classification schemata may vary across data sources and time. Clearly, this diversity of diagnostic schema will present problems to the researcher when data from different sources, or different historic times, must be reconciled or made comparable. Unfortunately, appropriate translation between diagnostic systems may not be possible in every instance. In such situations, collapsing diagnoses into more general categories may be the best solution. Moreover, given problems of diagnostic reliability, which will be discussed shortly, such a solution need not be seen as an unwelcome compromise as long as the general categories are not so broad as to be useless.

Diagnosis is a nominal level measure, having no underlying continuum of severity across diagnoses. Although there are diagnostic pairs that imply a continuum of severity (e.g., dysthymia is minor depression compared to major depression), there is controversy as to whether this is a quantitative or a qualitative difference. Although individuals may be measured as to the severity of their symptoms or disability, there is little justification for saying that schizophrenia per se is more severe than a major depression, or vice versa. Diagnoses must be applied with great caution when utilized cross-culturally and with children.

DIAGNOSTIC RELIABILITY

Diagnostic reliability remains an important consideration regardless of the particular classification schema used. Upon reading the literature on diagnostic reliability, the social scientist will become rapidly aware of several things. First, the reliability theory current in social science that focuses upon domain sampling and internal consistency is rarely examined in the psychiatric literature. Rather, issues of inter-observer reliability and test-retest reliability are emphasized. Second, published reliability estimates tend to be quite high for general diagnostic categories, but considerably lower for subtypes.

The major nosologies have all had extensive reliability research done on them. Spitzer, Endicott, and Robins (1975) report RDC reliabilities ranging from a low of .17 for depressive personality to a high of .93 for bipolar, manic. The DSM-III (American Psychiatric Association, 1980) details two studies done on the reliability of that schema prior to its final modification and publication. The second-phase study, yielding the higher reliability coefficients, reported an overall kappa of .72 for Axis I and .64 for Axis II. However, considerable differences were reported among kappas for major categories. In their comparison across nosologies, Gruenberg et al. (1985) found that the ICD had the lowest over all kappa value ($\kappa = .58$) of the four schemata studied. For subtypes of schizophrenia, DSM-III consistently had the highest reliability of the three major nosologies. The fourth nosology studied, the Tsuang and Winokur (1974) criteria, was consistently most reliable. Furthermore, as Dumont (1987) points out, in some studies high kappas are sometimes obtained only for diagnostic categories so broad as to be virtually useless for both clinician and researcher.

Unfortunately, inconsistent methodology confounds two conceptually distinct questions that are at issue here: the reliable application of information to a schema (criterion variance); and the reliability of the data to be applied (information variance). The first question is whether different clinicians use the classification schema in a consistent way. That is, will different diagnosticians yield different diagnoses, given the same data? Davis, Janicak, and Andriukaitis (1986) observe that using the nomenclature of a schema does not necessarily mean that the clinician (or other rater) followed the criteria for that diagnosis. Although this is obviously the case with a schema such as ICD-9, which does not have extensive detail, the same may be asked of the more descriptively detailed schemata such as DSM-III-R.

Winokur (Winokur, Zimmerman, & Cadoret, 1988) notes that given the same data, clinicians may disagree on the diagnosis because of differences in the interpretation of schema criteria. Although this was a problem in both the DSM-II and the RDC, it was most notable in the Feighner schema. Furthermore, Winokur suggests the possibility of systematic intercenter bias, which would be especially hazardous to research done at multiple sites. The second reliability issue focuses upon the source of the information used in the diagnostic process. Where there is wide variation in the method used to acquire information to be applied to the classification schema, one would expect poor reliability. Common clinical practice relies upon unstructured, open-ended interviews to gather data pertinent to the diagnostic process. Such data are unreplicable and unstandardized, rendering them unsuitable for most research purposes. Moreover, as Grove, Andreasen, McDonald-Scott, Keller, and Shapiro (1981) point out, most reliability studies not only do not clearly separate the application of criteria to a schema and the degree to which data acquisition is standardized, but they also do not control for the experience and training of the raters, and in the case of test-retest designs, the retest interval used, and the actual changes in the mental state of subjects/patients. Thus, the reliability of diagnosis is far from satisfactorily settled.

Interlude

The following is an example of how diagnostic inconsistency can impact even the simplest of research designs. Records of all patients who were referred through the continuity of care unit of a large public sector urban mental health system between 1985 and 1988 were examined. Patients were referred through this unit upon hospital discharge in order to be placed at an appropriate outpatient facility for follow-up care. Among the variables coded for each patient was the discharge diagnosis for each hospitalization. Of the 2,605 patients coded, 567 (21.8%) had records of multiple hospitalizations, ranging from 2 to 11 over the 3-year period. Considering just these 567, the diagnosis was changed at least once for 44.1% of the patients. Included in this group was a patient who, across five hospitalizations, had four different diagnoses. Moreover, 30% of the sample were given a different diagnosis *each time* they were hospitalized. The most striking case of diagnostic shift in this data base involved a man with a history of chronic schizophrenia spanning two decades. The patient was hospitalized due to an acute exacerbation of psychotic symptoms following the death of a parent. The discharge diagnosis was adjustment disorder with depressed mood. The attending psychiatrist responsible for follow-up care switched it back to chronic schizophrenia with acute exacerbation.

Were these discharges from a general hospital, the changing diagnoses would not be noteworthy. One could have heart surgery, followed a year later by cancer, for example. However, in psychiatry, diagnosis usually adheres to the general principal of one patient/one (Axis I) illness (Gruenberg, 1986). Individuals do not have schizophrenia one year and bipolar illness the next. Nevertheless, the diagnoses of a large proportion of patients in this data set appear to violate that principle. More than 38% of the patients had diagnoses that shifted between some functional psychosis and a nonpsychotic illness. Another 42% experienced diagnostic shifts within the major psychotic disorders, such as schizophrenia, schizoaffective, and atypical psychosis. Many shifts that indicated diagnostic uncertainty involved switches among schizophrenia, schizoaffective, and affective disorder diagnoses. Another 10% were changes involving organic brain disorders.

These data also provide an illustration of intercenter bias mentioned by Winokur et al. (1988). Restricting analysis to those patients who had experienced two hospitalizations, changes in diagnosis were crosstabulated with changes in discharging hospital. Significant differences were found ($\chi^2 = 4.028$; $df = 1$; $p < .05$) with a weak association indicated (Yule's Q = .21). Patients discharged twice from the same hospital were somewhat more likely to retain the same diagnosis. However, should a patient be discharged from two different hospitals, there was a nearly even chance that the diagnoses would be different.

Under these conditions, how does the researcher assign a diagnosis to the patient based upon the *written record*? Should one use the last diagnosis; or the modal diagnosis; or possibly avoid the entire issue by changing the unit of analysis from the patient to the discharge event?

GOLD STANDARDS AND DIAGNOSTIC MARKERS

The purpose of a marker is not necessarily to discover the biological cause for a psychiatric disorder, but to locate some characteristic that is always associated with the illness and is never seen in someone without the illness. To be able to measure or observe some trait or characteristic that is a necessary and sufficient condition for the presence of a specific psychopathology would significantly advance research on the mentally ill. The implementation of a medical model of diagnosis on the basis of laboratory reports of blood tests, CT scans, PET scans, and other imaging techniques would lift much of the uncertainty associated with making a psychiatric diagnosis. Unfortunately, brain imaging, although adding much to knowledge of functioning and structure in the brain (Andreasen, 1988), has not as yet yielded any tests that can serve as a gold standard for the diagnosis of mental disorder. Although genetic etiologies are hypothesized for a number of mental illness, markers have not been firmly established for any of them other than for Huntington's chorea (Shapiro, Comings, Jones, & Rimoin, 1986), a disease that can cause psychosis.

At the present time, organic brain disorders are one class of diagnosis most often made with the aid of physiological tests. Electroencephalograms (EEGs) and various imaging technologies are sometimes clinically helpful (Popkin, 1986). However, these techniques are considered useful but not definitive. The same may be said of the battery of neuropsychological tests. There are physiological markers for Alzheimer's disease, in the form of plaques in the brain, but since these can only be observed during autopsy (Rossor, 1984; Tomlinson, 1980), such a marker is of only limited research utility. Attempts to find necessary and sufficient markers for specific functional disorders have not yielded definitive results. Encouraging work has been done using the Dexamethasone Suppression Test for depression. However, as work has progressed on the DST, it appears that it is not specific to depression. Patients diagnosed with obsessional neurosis, schizophrenia, anorexia, and Alzheimer's have been found to show abnormal suppression as well (Winokur, 1986). Nevertheless, the procedure continues to capture much attention, as techniques to define optimal cutting points are developed in the psychiatric literature (see Hsiao, Bartko, & Potter, 1989; Mossman & Somoza, 1989). Among other possibilities being investigated are a sodium lactate test for panic disorder, rapid eye movement (REM) disturbances in the depressed (Kupfer, 1976; Winokur, 1986), and rheumatoid arthritis for schizophrenia (Eaton, 1986).

Many clinicians maintain that the clinical interview itself is the gold standard for collection of diagnostic data against which the validity of all other methods must be compared. However, for most research, the mental status examination given under typical clinical conditions is not an acceptable gold standard. Typically, clinical interviews are loosely structured, unstandardized, and dependent upon the skill, experience, and paradigmatic orientation of the interviewer. They are unreplicable and often poorly documented. Nevertheless, sensitivity and specificity of a potential marker or laboratory test are usually compared against the clinical interview. The unreliability of the clinical interview, however, sets upper limits upon the validity and reliability of any new diagnostic test (Hsiao et al., 1989). Winokur, Zimmerman, and Cadoret (1988) note that the results of DST testing have varying relationships to diagnosis, depending upon how diagnostic criteria are applied. In the absence of a true gold standard, researchers such as Klerman (1985) argue that the assessment of the validity of new instruments should be made in terms of agreement/disagreement or concordance/discordance with older measures, without implying that the older is a standard against which a new measure is compared. If there is low concordance, it could be due to the inadequacy of the older measure rather than the invalidity of the new.

DIAGNOSTIC INSTRUMENTATION

In the absence of reliable and valid markers, and in lieu of the clinical interview, researchers have developed an armamentarium of scales and interview schedules to use as diagnostic assessment instruments. Varying in the extent of coverage, some of these instruments are integrally tied into a specific diagnostic classification schema, although others are not. They all have a common purpose, however: to identify a case. Each attempts to determine if the respondent (patient) has a diagnosable mental illness. This distinguishes them from other types of instruments, which may generate data with regards to symptoms, but are not intended to yield a diagnosis.

The diagnostic instruments itemized in Table 3.2, although not comprising an exhaustive list, are used in research and have known psychometric

Table 3.2

Common Diagnostic Interview Instruments

Instrument	Author	Type	Schema Compatibility
Diagnostic Interview Schedule (DIS)	Robins et al., 1981	Structured	DSM-III RDC Feighner
Diagnostic Interview Schedule-R (DIS-R)	Robins, 1989	Structured	DSM-III-R RDC Feighner
Composite International Diagnostic Interview (CIDI)	Robins et al., 1988	Structured	DSM-III ICD-10
Structured Clinical Interview for DSM-III-R (SCID)	Spitzer & Williams, 1988	Semi-Structured	DSM-III
Renard Diagnostic Interview (RDI)	Helzer et al., 1981	Structured	Feighner
Schedule for Affective Disorders and Schizophrenia (SADS)	Endicott & Spitzer, 1978	Semi-Structured	RDC
Present State Examination (PSE)	Wing et al., 1974	Unstructured	ICD

properties. Typically, the standard against which the criterion-related validity of these instruments is judged is the clinical interview, with all its attending problems. Discriminant validity is dichotomized into test sensitivity and test specificity. High rates of false positives and false negatives are considered signs of instrument weakness and are differentially devalued, depending upon the consequences of a wrong identification. Sensitivity and specificity must be balanced in much the same way that the researcher must balance the costs of making Type I and Type II statistical errors. As with criterion-related validity, discriminant validity is usually ascertained by comparison with the clinical interview. The model of instrument reliability most commonly used is that of temporal consistency (using Cohen's kappa), rather than the domain sampling model (using Cronbach's coefficient alpha) current in the social sciences.

Diagnostic Interview Schedule

The Diagnostic Interview Schedule (DIS) series of interview schedules (Robins, Helzer, Croughan, & Ratcliff, 1981), created under the sponsorship of NIMH, were developed as case finding instruments to be used in epidemiological studies. Like their immediate predecessor, the Renard Diagnostic Interview (Helzer, Robins, Croughan, & Welner, 1981), the various editions of the DIS are highly structured, are closed-ended, and can be administered by trained interviewers with no prior mental health experience. The structured protocol makes the DIS simultaneously attractive to researchers and unattractive to clinicians. Substantively, the same results are obtained (for the measurement of depression) whether administered by face-to-face interview or by telephone (Wells, Burnam, Leake, & Robins, 1988). The DIS has been translated into several languages, including Spanish, German, and Chinese. Scoring can be done either manually or by computer software. Using the computer algorithm for scoring standardizes the way in which the obtained data are applied to the schema, thereby minimizing an important source of diagnostic unreliability. Although designed to cover 40 DSM-III diagnoses, the DIS also produces data sufficient for making diagnoses using the RDC and Feighner schemata. The DIS is capable of making both current and lifetime diagnoses, and some diagnoses can be made at the definite and probable levels of certainty. There are modified versions specifically for alcohol- and substance-abuse diagnoses (SAM) and for administering to children (DISC).

The instrument is complex to administer, having structured probes and skips. Interviewer training, which is strongly recommended by the distributors, is available as a 5-day program currently conducted in St. Louis, Missouri. Robins et al. (1981) suggest that the instrument takes between 45 and 75 minutes to administer. This estimate may be realistic for epidemiological samples where skips can be used liberally. However, the interview time for clinical samples will probably be much longer, since more probes and fewer skips would be typical.

Composite International Diagnostic Interview

The Composite International Diagnostic Interview (CIDI) is an instrument created by Robins, Wing, Wittchen, Helzer, Babor, Burke, Farmer, Jablenski, Pickens, Regier, Sartorius, & Towle (1988) specifically for cross-cultural epidemiologic studies. The instrument contains much overlap with the DIS and the Present State Examination (discussed below), but with modifications intended to make the questions less culturally specific. The validity and reliability of this instrument over a variety of settings has yet to be published.

Structured Clinical Interview

The Structured Clinical Interview for DSM-III-R (SCID) was developed by Spitzer and Williams (1988). The instrument differs from the DIS series in that it is designed for use by a clinician. Although structured, it contains many open-ended items and requires the use of clinical judgment in the choice of probes and skips before recording a response into a fixed choice format.

**Schedule for Affective Disorders
and Schizophrenia**

The Schedule for Affective Disorders and Schizophrenia (SADS) was developed as a companion to the RDC diagnostic nosology (Endicott & Spitzer, 1978). It has three forms: the basic; an -L version for lifetime diagnoses; and a -C version for changes over time. The SADS is less structured than the DIS and describes symptoms at their most severe manifestation, rather than describing symptoms at the time of the interview. The interview protocol yields information for more than 20 RDC diagnoses plus subtypes. There are two residual categories as well as two categories for no disorder. Its developers suggest a testing time of 1.5 to 2 hours (Endicott & Spitzer). Although most frequently used with patient populations, there has been some experience with the SADS in community settings (Vernon & Roberts, 1982; Weissman & Myers, 1978).

Present State Examination

The Present State Examination (PSE) developed by Wing, Cooper, and Sartorius (1974) is better suited as a clinical tool than as a research instrument. The interview protocol has been updated often since the 1960s, and can yield diagnoses compatible with the ICD schema, using a computer program, CATEGO. The instrument is seldom used today for research purposes, but did contribute to the development of the more structured instruments currently favored.

INSTRUMENTS MEASURING SYMPTOMS

Researchers studying *mental illness* use a wide array of scales and indexes. However, they are quite different from those used by researchers studying *mental health*. Most instruments for the study of mental health have been developed for nonclinical populations. Their content tends to focus upon stress, hassles, and personality types. One instrument that has been widely used in general psychosocial surveys is the Langner Scale (Langner 1962), a short, self-administered series of 22 questions measuring the level of emotional distress. The scale is biased toward somatic complaints, without the ability to screen out those not psychogenic in etiology (Weissman, Myers, & Ross, 1986b). The scale neither identifies cases, nor generates symptom clusters.

If one is studying the mentally ill, one must choose a scale of sufficient sensitivity at the extremes to capture variation. A scale that can discriminate between ill and non-ill persons may not be able to differentiate among degrees of illness found at the extremes. Instruments designed for general populations may yield uniformly extreme scores if used on a sample of mentally ill people. Conversely, since some scales (e.g., the Langner Scale) are designed to measure mild forms of mental distress, people with serious mental illness may score lower than people with less severe symptoms (Weissman et al., 1986b).

In contrast, many of the instruments for studying mental illness were initially created for clinical use, but have become part of the arsenal of research instrumentation. Many of these instruments are published scales. Because they are commercially printed and sold, their use requires permission from the holder of the copyright and sometimes the payment of a fee. The reader is advised to make appropriate inquiries prior to the use of such instruments.

There is a plethora of instruments that might be chosen to measure illness variables. Among these are a series of instruments that measure a broad range of symptoms clustered into several subscales. Examples include the self-administered MMPI, which is used with both general and ill samples. The Brief Psychiatric Rating Scale (Overall & Gorham, 1962) is an example of an instrument more often used with identified cases. Following a structured, open-ended protocol, two psychologists or psychiatrists concurrently interview but independently rate each patient (Research and Education Association, 1981).

The Symptom Checklist-90 (SCL-90) is an example of a compromise between the MMPI type and the BPRS type. Like the MMPI, the SCL-90 can be self-administered; but like the BPRS, it is much shorter (90 items) and historically has been used with patient samples, especially to measure response to medication. Like both the MMPI and the BPRS, it can be scored with a series of subscale scores. The SCL-90 has the advantage of being sensitive to changes over time. Its shorter length makes it more suitable for repeated measuring than longer instruments such as the MMPI.

Another class of instrument focuses upon narrower clusters of symptoms. There is a wide variety of clinical scales to measure level of depression (Hickey & Baer, 1988; Moran & Lambert, 1983). Foremost among them are the Beck, Ward, Mendelson, Mock, and Erbaugh (1961), the Zung (1965), and the modified Hamilton (I. Miller, Bishop, Norman, & Maddever, 1985) scales. There are also special scales suitable for use with children, such as the Children's Depression Inventory (CDI) (Benfield, Palmer, Pfefferbaum, & Stowe, 1988).

A symptom scale for depression that is in favor among social scientists is the Center for Epidemiologic Studies Depression Scale (CES-D), developed by Radloff (1977) for use with general populations. It is a 20-question, self-administered instrument with items drawn from other established scales (Myers & Weissman, 1980). It is highly reliable and of known discriminant validity, though some maintain that it is uncertain whether the CES-D taps the domain of depression, or a more general domain of psychological distress (Devins & Orme, 1985). Myers and Weissman suggest a cut-off score of 16 to identify a case of major depression that is purported to be comparable to a case as defined by the SADS/RDC criteria. They also suggest that compared to diagnoses made using the SADS/RDC method, the CES-D yields a low rate of false positives, but a rather high rate of false negatives (36.4% for major depression and 77% for minor depression). These findings suggest that instruments designed to measure the extent of symptoms do not identify cases the same as instruments designed to yield diagnoses.

Similarly, there are many scales for anxiety, alcohol and substance abuse, and various other symptom clusters. It is beyond the scope of this volume to elaborate upon all of them. However, available to the researcher are a number of instrument anthologies that can be of assistance. Among these are: *The Handbook of Psychiatric Rating Scales* (Research and Education Association, 1981); *Test Critiques* (Keyser & Sweetland, 1985); and *Measures for Clinical Practice* (Corcoran & Fischer, 1987).

Some suggestions about instrumentation decisions are now in order. The first recommendation is to use an instrument already developed that has known validity and reliability, rather than attempting to develop a new one. This will be more readily acceptable to readers than an unfamiliar instrument and will make new findings interpretable in light of previous research.

Choosing among the wide assortment of available instruments is a crucial task, albeit a difficult one. There are two obvious schools of instrument design. One, typified by the instruments developed by Lee Robins, utilizes highly structured formats that can be administered by personnel trained in interviewing but not trained as clinicians. The other school, typified by the work of Spitzer and Endicott, offers less-structured formats that are best administered by personnel having clinical and well as research training. Although the styles have been tending somewhat to converge recently (P. Cohen, 1988), with some elements of structure and open-ended formats present in both, differences remain. The researcher will make a selection based upon his or her own methodological preferences for degree of interview structure. Beyond this, matters of available personnel, sample sizes, cost, and purpose of the project must be considered. The potential audience also should be anticipated. Reviewers vary in their instrumentation preferences, and these are reflected in differential acceptance by journals. Thus, the researcher must target journals for publication even in the beginning stages of planning, so that instruments are chosen that will be compatible with the preferences of the chosen audience.

One must decide whether a measure of diagnosis or a measure of symptoms is desired. Much has been said already about the conceptual and measurement problems associated with diagnosis. Unless one's theory specifically requires a measurement of diagnosis, which is obtained independently of the routine clinical practice, measuring symptoms may be more appropriate. The instruments are generally shorter and more focused. They tend to have higher reliability with clearer content or construct validation. They are also better suited for measuring patient change over time. However, as noted previously, sometimes the use of diagnosis is unavoidable due to the demands and expectations of others on the research team and / or targeted audiences. The researcher may ultimately decide that one instrument alone is not adequate, that a variety of instrumentation approaches is needed. Such a design would maximize the strengths of each of the types of instruments and would yield results with validity superior to that obtained by a single method design.

4

Special Problems in Design

When conducting research on persons with mental illness, methodologists have at their disposal the range of designs familiar to social science: the sample survey using either questionnaires or interviews, experimental and quasi-experimental designs, participant observation, structured observations, and so forth. It is not the purpose of this chapter to explain the basic designs; that is available in any good research methods text. The beginning researcher can refer to books such as Babbie's (1989) basic methodology textbook for general methodological guidance or to such books as Grady and Wallston (1988) for methodological guidance with specific reference to medical settings. Rather than repeat the basic tenets of design, this chapter will examine some problems encountered in the translation of these designs to studies of the mentally ill.

POPULATIONS AND SAMPLING FRAMES

The strength and utility of a study start with the definition of the study population. Unless that population and its attendant sampling frame can yield a sample that is representative of and generalizable to the population of interest, interpretation of data will be limited. With some exceptions, research in psychiatry could be criticized because it tends to be restricted to samples of patients in treatment without adequate comparisons with nonclinical populations. Patient samples may be appropriate for some research, such as treatment outcome studies. However, sampling frames limited to patients cannot be used to determine etiology or differential risk factors, because they are not representative of a general population and so tend to elevate rates of symptoms. The persistent use of these limited samples is due at least in part to the clinical interests of the psychiatrist/researcher and to the accessibility of treatment populations.

Conversely, behavioral scientists most often use samples drawn from general populations. This works well when studying the distress of individuals who are not clinical cases. However, community samples serve less well when studying people who have a mental illness, or who are defined as a case. Although lifetime prevalence for mental illness is 25% (Myers et al., 1984), specific illness categories are statistically rare events. Thus, people identified as having schizophrenia, which has a prevalence of approximately 1% of the population, are inefficiently studied, using samples of the general population. The most reasonable alternative to the general sample is to use a clinical sample. Among persons in treatment, persons with diagnoses of schizophrenia are not particularly rare events and may be found in very high proportions in some treatment settings. However, bias is introduced since the population of persons in treatment for schizophrenia is but a subset of all persons meeting the schizophrenia criteria. Unfortunately, untreated cases can be extremely difficult to locate. An illustration of the impact of this issue can be drawn from the controversy in the literature regarding the rate of mental illness among the homeless. Studies that track persons in psychiatric treatment yield lower rates of mental illness than samples that track through health care facilities other than psychiatric ones (Wright, 1988). This is because a significant proportion of people who present at a medical clinic will also have psychiatric disorders for which they do not seek treatment at a mental health clinic. Thus, each sampling method introduces its own set of biases, including that of differential rates of help-seeking at each type of facility.

Sampling within a population of cases has its own problems. When there are people sampled who, at a specified time, have some mental illness, they will have acquired their illnesses at different points. If a particular illness tends to lead to an early death (e.g., suicide for literal death or possibly subject mortality created by hospitalization), there is a reduced probability of including cases having that early-death illness in the sample (Neyman, 1955). An example is supplied by Vernon and Roberts (1982), who found that relying upon a community sample led to an underestimation of the rates of severe disorders, because some of the severely disordered were hospitalized at the time of the survey. Furthermore, since rates of hospitalization vary by social characteristics, such as race and ethnicity, as well as the severity of illness, a community sample not only underestimates the rates of illness but also distorts the relationship between illness and ethnicity.

Likewise, differential attrition rates can seriously affect a sample drawn for a retrospective study (Neyman). Hence, if an illness is of short duration, there will be an under-inclusion of persons having that illness relative to those having a chronic illness.

Feinstein (1985) suggests another issue raised by using hospitalized patients as a sampling frame: an issue that he calls Berkson's bias. Berkson (1946) noted that differential hospitalization rates may distort associations between illnesses and/or between illness and patient characteristics. People with two illnesses are more likely to be hospitalized than people with one illness. If the rate of hospitalization varies for the two illnesses, when a hospitalized population is sampled, the concurrent prevalence rate of illness is likely to be higher than would be representative in the community. Where the likelihood of hospital referral is affected by the co-occurrence of two illnesses, the occurrence of the illness in the hospital sample may be considerably higher than in the community population. Thus, Berkson's bias may operate with the "dual diagnosis" psychiatric patient (e.g., patients with substance abuse co-occurring with another mental illness).

Once an appropriate sampling frame is established, selection of actual subjects may proceed. Although some variety of random or probabilistic sampling is preferred for statistical reasons, there may be instances where this is not possible. Goetz and LeCompte (1984) point out situations where other forms of selection may be mandated, especially in ethnographic and other qualitative designs. Criterion-based selection may be indicated when the study is exploratory and when one task of the research is to define the boundaries of the population of interest.

Other instances for purposive selection occur when only a small number of population characteristics are considered relevant to a study (Goetz & LeCompte). Researchers specify inclusionary and exclusionary criteria that are applied to individuals (usually patients) who are available as potential study participants. These criteria are used in an attempt to develop a homogeneous subject pool from which random assignment to experimental groups is made. There is no attempt to make the subject pool representative of a general population, or even representative of a clinical population. This type of criterion-based selection is typical of clinical trials and other biomedical experimental research.

CASE IDENTIFICATION

As discussed previously, much attention is focused upon the identification and counting of cases. In particular, a basic epidemiological task is the estimation of incidence and prevalence of cases of mental illness. Incidence refers to the frequency or rate of *new* cases developed in a population during a specific time period. Prevalence is the frequency or rate of extant cases (including new and preexisting) in the population at a particular time (Lilienfeld & Lilienfeld, 1980). There are three types of prevalence: point, period, and lifetime. Estimates of point prevalence are concerned with the number of cases at a particular point in time, usually on some specified day or during a specified week. Period prevalence is an estimate of cases during some longer time range, such as a month or a year. Lifetime prevalence is the number of persons who have been cases (or had the illness) at any time during their lives. Although incidence, point prevalence, and period prevalence are usually measured using data on the subjects' current status, lifetime prevalence is usually measured by the subjects' retrospective recall. Period and lifetime prevalences are more often used in psychiatric epidemiology than are point prevalence or incidence (Schwab & Schwab, 1978).

Although prevalence and incidence studies may be of somewhat less interest to the behavioral scientist than they are to the psychiatric epidemiologist, social scientists have made contributions in that area. Estimated prevalence of mental illness among the homeless, discussed above, is but one example. Furthermore, case identification is often a first step in studies of etiology, identification of risk factors, and other hypothesis-testing research.

In addition to the measurement of caseness, there are issues of design of case identification studies. The most important centers on the minimization of false negatives and false positives. Assuming that no one measure of caseness will have perfect sensitivity and perfect specificity, the ideal design for case finding will include techniques to identify the incorrectly classified individuals. Dohrenwend (1983) advocates a multistage-multimethod design for epidemiologic and case identification studies. Such a method entails the use of an initial screening instrument, followed by at least two additional stages, each using a different instrument. After the initial step, subjects are separated into probable cases and probable noncases. Then, using a more detailed, unstructured protocol, an additional instrument would be administered. Where there is no disagreement between stage one and stage two, the individual would be classified as either a true positive or a true negative, depending upon the consistent results of both tests. Where there is disagreement, the third stage would be activated. Using even more detailed instruments, perhaps with clinical examination and/or informant interviewing, false positives and false negatives would then be identified. Studies using this methodology are consistent with Campbell and Fiske's (1959) multitrait-multimethod matrix design to maximize validity.

LONGITUDINAL DESIGNS

The design of longitudinal studies must anticipate disruptions in the implementation over which the researcher may have no control. In particular, allowances must be made for any cyclical effects known to occur with the patient's illness, as will be detailed in Chapter 5. Longitudinal designs must be of sufficient length to allow for these periodicities.

Furthermore, allowances must be made for patients shifting between inpatient and outpatient status. A common example is the case in which one is testing the efficacy of an outpatient intervention. How are rehospitalized subjects to be counted? Some studies have actually dropped them from the study because of the unavailability of the rehospitalized for completing the intervention or for completing data collection. However, since rehospitalization is sometimes due to the failure of outpatient treatment, the success rate of the intervention is inflated by the deletion of the failures.

Other researchers may not consider hospitalization as an intervention failure or the end of participation in an outpatient study. Nevertheless, there must be provision made for such events in the design. With short-term hospitalizations common, the researcher must consider how to handle a rehospitalization during the study period. Should such patients be reentered into the project upon discharge? Will these patients have so much missing data that they will be eliminated from analysis, even if not intentionally disqualified by the study? How will that affect the outcome of the study? If subjects are dropped from the study in a random manner because of rehospitalization or because of missing data, they may not affect results. But if subjects are deleted due to differential effectiveness of the intervention, or to variables associated with intervention effectiveness, their absence will produce inaccurate rates of effect (Feinstein, 1985).

Similarly, longitudinal studies of inpatients must consider whether the expected length of hospitalization will be sufficient for completion of the data collection. If post-discharge follow-up is planned, multiple strategies may be needed for tracking patients. Tracing through kin, friends, and aftercare treatment facilities are three possible routes to the location of discharged patients.

EXPERIMENTAL DESIGNS

The prototypical research in biomedicine uses the classic experimental design with its emphasis upon randomization, controls, and blinding. Designs often include multiple treatments with crossovers and other variations. Such designs are commonly employed in clinical trials studies; that is, evaluations of the efficacy of pharmacologic interventions are frequent research topics. In addition, questions involving the outcome of psychotherapies, or the evaluation of the impact of system changes, suggest experimental designs. Feinstein's (1985) book is a detailed exposition of biomedical research methodologies, with an emphasis upon experimentation that many will find helpful.

Randomization

One need not read far in biomedical methodology texts before realizing that classic experimental design is not always directly translatable into methods for researching the mentally ill, even in a clinical setting. For example, randomization, an essential component of the true experiment, is often impossible to implement. It may be possible to assemble a pool of alcohol abusers and then randomly assign them into different treatment groups. However, it is not possible to collect a pool of subjects, and randomly assign them into a one group who will abuse alcohol and another group who will not, in order to induce secondary organic disorders. Other examples of studies where randomization is usually impossible are those natural field experiments that occur with organization change or system innovation. In these situations, selection into groups is predetermined by the individual's prior place in the system and is not amenable to randomization.

Control Groups

The second bulwark of the experimental design is the control group. Although some psychiatric researchers will still use the subject as his or her own control, such a design is usually considered weak by medical researchers (Feinstein, 1985), psychiatric researchers (American Psychiatric Association Commission on Psychotherapies, 1982), and behavioral scientists (Campbell & Stanley, 1963). Rather, one must create an independent group, designated as a control, that does not receive the experimental treatment and to which the experimental treatment group can be compared along the critical variables. In a drug study the control group typically is given a placebo (i.e., an inert substance indistinguishable from the experimental drug in appearance and dose regimen; examples include administering sugar pills and injections of saline solution) as a substitute for the experimental medication. The purpose of the placebo is to enable the researcher to separate changes in the patient's condition due to the objective effects of the medication from changes due to psychological effects of reduced fears, raised expectations, and self-fulfilling prophecies.

When the experimental treatment is not pharmacological, the concept of the sugar pill placebo is translated into some theoretically neutral, inactive, or nonspecific (i.e., general to any therapeutic situation) factor such as attention. However, in dealing with the mentally ill, it is sometimes unknown precisely what will be therapeutic and what will not (American Psychiatric Association Commission on Psychotherapies, 1982). It is possible that mere attention may be therapeutic and thus may elicit a change in some controls. At the very least, it changes the expectations of patients/subjects in the control groups and may even evoke trust in the therapeutic situation (Strayhorn, 1987). Furthermore, Strayhorn argues that the nonspecific treatment in the placebo control group is merely a set of undefined, unmeasured psychological factors, which should be defined and systematically measured for a comparison with the defined psychological factors that are comprised in the treatment being tested in the experiment.

An alternative to using a placebo or attention control is to use completely untouched or untreated controls, who are merely observed or measured for baseline and post-test data. Usually these subjects are people who initially came seeking some type of care and entered the study with that expectation. Patients/subjects assigned to untreated control groups tend to seek help elsewhere when it is not forthcoming from the research site. Thus, they are either lost to the study or, if they remain enrolled in the study, they may react to treatments given elsewhere, which are unknown to the researcher and may have a confounding effect upon the experimental results (American Psychiatric Association Commission on Psychotherapies, 1982). This design is difficult to maintain unless the subjects are institutionalized and can be monitored throughout the study period. Furthermore, using untreated controls raises ethical concerns that will be discussed shortly.

Rather than assigning patients/subjects to no-treatment groups during randomization, no-treatment controls are sometimes drawn from either treatment dropout lists or treatment waiting lists (American Psychiatric Association Commission on Psychotherapies, 1982). Dropouts would be those patients who initially sought treatment, but then left so early in the screening or therapy stage that they are considered untreated. Early dropouts are extremely commonplace and thus would probably be available in sufficient numbers to form a control group. The percentage of people who drop out after the first visit ranges from 20% to 57%, while the percentage who drop out after no more than four visits ranges from 31% to 56% (Baekeland & Lundwall, 1975). However, there is a considerable literature that documents the many ways in which dropouts differ from those who stay in treatment. Because of differential dropout rates by diagnosis, age, socioeconomic status, and other psychosocial variables, controls drawn from dropouts would introduce prohibitive biases not obviated by random sampling within the dropout list.

The waiting list is a somewhat better candidate as a source for untreated controls. A natural part of many treatment facilities, the waiting list offers a pool of people who seek care and are not too likely to seek help elsewhere, at least during short waits. However, the researcher must be certain that waiting list candidates are, in fact, no different from those already in treatment. If there is triage screening prior to assignment to the waiting list, it is likely that waiting list individuals will differ from treated patients along some dimensions: type or severity of illness, financial status, clinical interest in the case, or organizationally mandated priorities. These differences will create nonequivalent study groups. One must learn whether control subjects are obtaining treatment elsewhere while on the waiting list. This is particularly important if the wait is a long one, as could be the case with some longitudinal designs, since the opportunities to enter treatment elsewhere while waiting for treatment at the research site are greater.

Alternatives to Untreated Controls

When one studies clinical populations, using untreated controls becomes problematic because of the ethical implications of withholding needed treatment. With clinicians generally committed to the value of providing treatment, it may be difficult to obtain clinical cooperation for a study with control groups in the design. Indeed, this is an issue whether the control group is scheduled to receive attention, some other placebo, or nothing at all. Another relevant ethical issue is highlighted by Strayhorn's (1987) critique of the practice of deceiving study subjects in placebo control groups for intervention outcome studies and other psychosocial research on clinical samples. He claims that whereas the concept of a "sugar pill" is easily understood and accepted by potential subjects in a drug study, the concept of an inert or useless therapy is less likely to be accepted by a psychiatric subject. Thus, researchers may be forced into utilizing more deception in describing the inert control in a nonpharmacological intervention study than might be ethically defensible.

Although a control group is mandated in experimentation, totally untreated and/or placebo groups are not. Rather than a placebo, the control group may receive an efficacious alternative treatment. Often the alternative used is the current standard of practice, which is compared to the new technique being given to the experimental group. The null hypothesis changes from one of no effect, to one of no difference from the effect of the current standard treatment. Strayhorn also suggests the use of "minimal but useful treatment" (p. 278) as a control. This would entail the use of some inexpensive treatment that was expected to be mildly beneficial to some controls. However, this does render the design less sensitive to detecting small effects. Strayhorn also suggests the decomposition of the experimental treatment into several components and the administering of a different combination of those components to various comparison groups.

The crossover design is another type of control common in medical experiments. Two or more experimental treatments are switched partway through the experiment in a counterbalanced design: Those getting treatment A next receive treatment B, and vice versa. This design is successful when no treatment is so powerful that it produces extreme scores subject to regression effects (American Psychiatric Association Commission on Psychotherapies, 1982). However, possible order main effects and order-treatment interaction effects be must examined carefully. In addition, as Campbell and Stanley (1963) point out, counterbalanced designs may be subject to complex interactions between selection and maturation effects, which may be salient when subjects having episodic illnesses are selected at specific symptom stages.

Beyond the issues of ethics, subject availability, and elimination of undesired confounding effects, a factor to consider is how the selection of control groups will influence sample size (Strayhorn, 1987). A design that compares an experimental treatment with no treatment will need fewer subjects than a design that compares an experimental treatment, with the current standard of care as the control. In the former case, the experimental treatment need only produce modest change for the effect size (i.e., the difference between the experimental and control groups) to be statistically significant at a given probability level and power. In the latter case, the new treatment must show itself to be superior to a standard treatment already shown to be efficacious. Thus, the effect size will probably be smaller, necessitating a larger sample size in order to achieve statistical significance (Lipsey, 1990).

Blinding

The third bulwark of the experimental design, especially as it is used in medical research, is blinding. In a single-blind design, patients/subjects do not know (are blind to) whether they have been placed in the control or the experimental group. In that way, reactive effects and subject biases are minimized. In a study of medication efficacy, placebo pills would be used that appear identical to the drug under study and are administered using an identical dosage regimen so that the subjects will not know whether they are receiving an active or inert substance.

The single-blind design is rarely adequate. Most studies also endeavor to keep the clinicians blind to minimize their reactivity and expectation effects. Thus the double-blind design is one in which neither the patient nor the clinician knows whether the placebo or the active treatment is actually being administered. In such cases, there is usually allowance made for breaking the blinding code in the event of a medical emergency. The double-blind experiment is thought to remove most reactive bias in the patient-doctor dyad. Nevertheless, good designs should go one step further and impose a third blind upon the rater or data collector if he or she is different from the clinician.

Blinded designs are possible when the clinical trials involve the use of a medication that can have a placebo made that is identical in appearance to the active treatment. However, the experiments of treatment outcomes for the mentally ill are often of types that are difficult to blind. Where the experimental treatment involves psychotherapy or behavioral therapies, clinicians cannot be blind as to which kind of treatment is being dispensed since they are active components of that treatment. Nor can the patient always be kept blind. If an individual has been in treatment previously, it will be evident if a different treatment is being used. Similarly, waiting room socializing may suggest to a patient/subject that different therapies are being used. If multiple research sites are possible, then each site could be used for a different treatment to minimize contamination effects among patients. Unfortunately, multiple sites introduce other sources of bias (Kraemer, Pruyn, Gibbons, Greenshouse, Grochocinski, Waternaux, & Kupfer, 1987); one must expand the design to include additional controls for a potential site effect as well. Sometimes the only blind that can be imposed is upon the independent rater. Nevertheless, to whatever extent blinding can be imposed, it should be done in order to strengthen the design.

Although the classic experimental design has utility in research on the mentally ill, very often the research question suggests an experimental format resembling less the clinical research typical in biomedicine and more the forms useful in the social, psychological, and education arenas. At such times, methodologists should consider appropriate alternative designs. These include quasi-experimental methods, such as those detailed by Cook and Campbell (1979). Selection of an appropriate quasi-experimental design may be more defensible than attempting to squeeze a study into a medical model of experimentation.

PARTICIPANT OBSERVATION

Although the focus of this book is on quantitative methods, the use of qualitative methods, specifically participant observation (P.O.), requires some attention. Unfortunately, there is less methodological literature to guide the researcher doing participant observation of the mentally ill than there is for the quantitative researcher. However, general guides such as Jorgensen's (1989) may be helpful.

The participant observation method is normally used when the research question is qualitative and concerns the world of the actor: "the meanings, concepts, definitions, characteristics, metaphors, symbols, and descriptions of things" (Berg, 1989, p. 2). It is closely associated with anthropological ethnography and is holistic in its approach to describing cultures (Goetz & LeCompte, 1984) and culturally shaped behaviors. P.O. need not be totally phenomenological as Berg contends, but may rely upon categories generated by the researcher to frame the descriptions and analysis (Vidich, 1955). Nevertheless, in sociology the method is commonly, albeit not exclusively, linked to the theoretical approaches of symbolic interactionism.

However, Rosenberg (1984) contends that, from a symbolic interactionist perspective, what defines an insane (or psychotic) behavior is the inability of the observer to take the role of or understand the viewpoint of the actor. Accepting this definition potentially puts the participant observer in an untenable situation. If successful observation rests upon understanding the actor's motives and the actor's world, then P.O. is impossible to do with the seriously mentally ill.

Although this is an extreme interpretation of Rosenberg's argument, it is valuable insofar as it should raise a crucial question to the researcher planning an ethnographic study of the mentally ill. Can an observer have an empathetic understanding of the symptoms of mental illness?

Over the years that question has been considered with varying degrees of explicitness. In his preface to Asylums, Goffman's (1961) concern with empathy was expressed as a caveat that his view is that of a middle-class male who may not have experienced the hospital as lower-class patients do. Interestingly, he does not extend that caveat to the fact that the researcher also is not psychotic, and thus may not have been able to experience the hospital in the same way that a psychotic person may have experienced it. Perhaps this omission reflected Goffman's theoretical perspective challenging the existence of mental illness independent of the institutional syndrome that he describes in the book.

Twenty years after Goffman, Estroff (1981) confronted the empathy question more directly. Although explicitly working from a symbolic interactionist paradigm, Estroff warned of the personal danger she perceived in attempting to empathize too closely with her outpatient respondents, and advised that "the field worker in the psychiatric world must constantly guard against passages into a new reality" (p. 21). That view implies that deep empathy is difficult and decidedly undesirable if the researcher wishes to maintain an even mental state.

Despite the theoretical and personal problems associated with empathy, there are reasons to adopt a more moderate tone with respect to the possibility of doing participant observation among the mentally ill. Estroff suggests that deep empathy may be neither necessary nor desired. In fact, S. Miller (1952) maintained that excessive rapport within any field setting can compromise the quality of the data. Moreover, some empathy with the mentally ill should be possible. Unless the subject is in an acutely psychotic state, not all behaviors displayed are "crazy." If a person diagnosed with mental illness is in a stable, remitted condition, most behaviors will appear predominantly "sane" and understandable. This suggests that empathetic P.O. may be possible when the subjects are symptomatically stable.

Nevertheless, when dealing with a total individual the observer must be able to differentiate behaviors that are understandable (i.e., sane) from those that are not (i.e., insane). Such a differentiation may be difficult to make. Do apparently sane behaviors necessarily carry the same meaning for the observers as for the actor? Conversely, when a behavior is not understandable, is it necessarily "insane behavior" in that it defies role-taking by anyone, or are there empathic deficiencies in the observer that another observer may not have? Furthermore, the researcher must have some way of distinguishing between shared views or a subculture of the mentally ill, and unique realities experienced only by a particular informant.

As with any fieldwork of this type, one must seriously consider the social role to be adopted by the researcher. Although complete participation through total and covert immersion in the setting may seem attractive, most experienced field researchers reject this role (Hammersley & Atkinson, 1983), favoring a more open approach. Socially marginal roles, such as "participant as observer" or "observer as participant" (Junker, 1960), are ultimately less limiting and permit subtle role changes as the research progresses. Hence, the researcher is advised to enter the scene with identity known. Even so, there may be misinterpretations of the researcher's role, and even the possible incorporation of the observer into a subject's delusional system. However, covert entry is subject to even greater misinterpretation, even to the point of the observer's being unable to exit the scene when desired. This occurred in the Rosenhan (1973) study, in which researchers who were committed incognito to a psychiatric hospital had difficulty leaving at the conclusion of the fieldwork.

Furthermore, one should consider using a research team rather than being a lone observer. A team can provide interpretation checks. It will allow for a wider net of informants, making possible the differentiation between a shared culture and an idiosyncratic reality. Although these are issues facing all ethnographers to some degree, the severity and immediacy of these problems are greater when researching the mentally ill.

5

The Mentally Ill as Respondents

It is unrealistic to expect that interview or questionnaire data will be completely accurate, regardless of the population sampled. Even among nonpsychiatric medical patients there are data errors from a variety of sources, including the hiding of facts from care providers (DiMatteo & Friedman, 1982), and the censoring of information given in medical interviews (Stimson & Webb, 1989). Cannell, Oksenberg, and Converse (1977) found discrepancies when comparing medical patient responses with their written medical records. Hospital episodes, physician visits, and number of medical conditions were underreported. Thus, researchers should normally expect some respondent-generated error to be present in interview data. However, when interviewing persons with mental illness, there may be additional error due to the nature of this special population. This chapter will focus upon how symptoms of mental illness may impact the research process when data are collected directly from an individual said to be mentally ill.

CHARACTERISTICS OF SERIOUS MENTAL ILLNESS

As with any classification of people, there is a danger of oversimplifying a heterogeneous assortment of characteristics of the mentally ill into an appearance of homogeneity. Thus, it is important to understand that not all mentally ill persons exhibit all the characteristics to be described, and that considerable behavioral and symptomatic heterogeneity exists even within a diagnostic category. Furthermore, different levels of functioning, of educational background, of intelligence, of income, as well as different racial/ethnic backgrounds contribute to diversity among the mentally ill, just as within a general population.

Clinical Symptoms

Depression: So prevalent is depression that it is sometimes called "the common cold of psychiatric disorders" (Charney & Weissman, 1988, p. 45). Not only is depression common relative to schizophrenia, but it is also often secondary to other mental illnesses (e.g., eating disorders, panic disorders, personality disorders, and substance abuse), and to many medical disorders (e.g., cancer, endocrine disorders, and cardiovascular disease) (Cameron, 1987). With the prevalence of depressive symptoms estimated between 13% and 20% of the general population, the researcher needs to be aware of how symptoms associated with depression can be significant impediments to data gathering.

Common symptoms of depression include: depressed mood, but not always sadness; loss of interest; anxiety; psychomotor retardation; and lack of energy (Hamilton, 1982). There is often change in cognitive functioning, feelings of guilt, helplessness, and hopelessness. Thus, it may be difficult to motivate the depressed person to participate in a study. More time and assistance may be required to complete an interview or questionnaire than would normally be the case.

Dementia: Dementia can be a more serious impediment to data quality than depression. More common in the elderly than in other age groups, dementia is an organic mental disorder that involves significant impairment of cognitive functioning, including profound memory loss eventually affecting both short- and long-term memory (Popkin, 1986). There may also be problems with abstract thinking, delusions, loss of interest, and increased distractibility (Popkin). An individual with significant dementia is probably not an appropriate respondent for an interview.

Psychosis: The decision about the appropriateness of interviewing a psychotic patient is formidable. Psychosis is defined as "any major mental disorder of organic or emotional origin marked by derangement of personality and loss of contact with reality, often with delusions, hallucinations, or illusions" (*Dorland's Medical Dictionary,* 1980, p. 568). Schizophrenia, paranoid disorder, bipolar disorder (manic-depressive illness), and some major depressions are psychotic illnesses. Typical psychotic symptoms likely to interfere with the research process will be mentioned briefly. However, it is beyond the scope of this chapter to describe thoroughly all the probable symptoms. Torrey (1988), and Birchwood,

Hallett, and Preston (1989) should be consulted for more complete descriptions.

It is very difficult to establish rapport with the psychotic person (Carpenter & Hanlon, 1986). The difficulty works two ways: It is difficult for the researcher to develop empathy with the psychotic experience, and the psychotic patient has difficulty forming social relationships. Psychotic patients are often fearful, supersensitive, and particularly responsive to nonverbal cues. In addition, lack of social skills and low levels of social functioning may make it difficult for subjects to keep appointments for a study, especially if travel away from home to an interviewing office is required.

Persons with a mental illness may also deny its existence. This may be a realistic attempt to avoid the stigma associated with mental illness (Eaton, 1986; C. Weiss, 1975), especially in the workplace or other nonclinical environment. Alternatively, denial is sometimes a symptom of the illness itself (Torrey). While observing an intake procedure at an outpatient clinic, I heard a patient, who had just been discharged from a psychiatric hospital, say that she did not think she had a mental illness, nor did she know she had been in a mental hospital until she was about ready to leave. She thought she had been hospitalized for an infected knee. In this case, denial means that a researcher would have had difficulty learning from that patient the medical definition of her problem.

People with major psychoses sometimes suffer time distortions. An example of this occurred when an outpatient, showing his lush vegetable garden from which he was about to harvest some spinach, claimed that he had planted it just 2 days before. Time distortion will have clear ramifications during interviews with questions that have a temporal reference. Even more critical are difficulties obtaining basic socio-demographic data. Age disorientation seems a particular problem among schizophrenics (Crow, 1990). Some 25% of institutionalized schizophrenics consistently underestimate their age, sometimes by 20 years or more (Stevens, Crow, Bowman, & Coles, 1978). A secondary source of information can verify some suspect data.

Another common symptom is limited attention span (Birchwood et al., 1989), along with either listlessness or restlessness. An inability to concentrate on a task suggests that the researcher must keep interviews brief, or hold several sessions with the respondent. A setting that is neither stimulating nor distracting would also be indicated.

Some psychoses involve delusions, which are fixed, false beliefs. Persons who have a manic-depressive psychosis will usually have grandiose delusions (exaggerated belief in their own importance or power) (Stokes, 1988); whereas people with schizophrenia often have persecutory delusions (belief that they are in unrealistic danger or are being treated with malevolence). Patients may incorporate the researcher into delusions by developing their own explanations for the researcher's questions that may relate more to the nature of the delusion than to the explanation and reassurances provided by the scientist. For example, a person with paranoid or persecutory delusions may believe the researcher is collecting information to be given to the surveillance agency, despite informed consents and letters of introduction. The interviewer should not directly confront the respondent regarding the reality of the delusional system, but should avoid that area of content.

A psychotic thought disorder also means that the respondent has difficulty interpreting abstract ideas, long sentences, or colloquialisms (Rosenbaum, 1970). The mode of expression may also be characterized by disconnectedness, vague or remote connections among adjacent statements, neologisms (invented idiosyncratic words), and poverty of speech and/or speech content (Birchwood et al., 1989; Torrey, 1988). As Torrey (p. 36) described, "the listener hears all the words, which may be almost correct, but at the end of the sentence or paragraph realizes that it doesn't 'make sense'." The manic person may manifest pressured speech, loud and persistent. Stokes notes that during a manic episode, conversation may become increasingly intimate, with uninvited familiarity. Any of these symptoms could be disconcerting to an unprepared interviewer.

Incoherence and illogicality may be encountered in the form of unusual answers to questions. One type is the deviance response tendency noted by Nunnally (1978), whereby a respondent makes an uncommon response to closed-ended questions. In this instance, uncommon responses may be indicative of particular personality traits and/or illnesses or may be nearly random responses on tests and inventories. Such deviant responses are not a function of the measurement instrument and cannot be eliminated by revising the instrument.

Symptoms of a thought disorder can become obvious with another type of incoherence or illogicality: bizarre answers to open-ended instruments. Instances of bizarre answers are not usually reported in the literature. However, in their study of chronically ill outpatients' knowledge about reproduction and sexually transmitted disease, Coverdale and Aruffo (1989) report that although 30% of their respondents gave one or more bizarre comments, 14% gave more than one bizarre answer.

Eisen, Grob, and Klein (1986) report that 3% of their subjects were "unable to respond appropriately" (p. 167).

Interlude

It is relatively easy to identify unusual answers when the instrument requires the respondent to agree or disagree with a specific statement, such as the MMPI item: "My soul sometimes leaves my body." However, when questions require an open-ended response, it is sometimes more difficult to judge whether a response is the result of either poor education or a different but essentially rational way of viewing the world, or whether the response is truly bizarre. The researcher must develop clear coding rules. Clinicians of a psychoanalytical orientation may argue that all verbalizations have meaning and logic; one only has to dig deeply enough into the subconscious to interpret even the most unusual statement (Rosenbaum, 1970). However, the researcher would be wise not either to overinterpret a response or utilize many logical steps to make sense of apparently illogical statements.

Consider the following examples of responses given by four outpatients in the Coverdale and Aruffo (1989) data.

Q. What other ways can you catch AIDS?
A. By wearing other peoples' clothes and drinking from another's cup or eating from his plate.

This should be considered merely misinformation (as the researchers did), rather than a bizarre response.

Q. What other ways can you catch AIDS?
A. Germs. Clam Chops.

The last part of this response should be judged as bizarre.

Q. What are the advantages of having children?
A. Load the dishwasher. Transfusions.

This response was coded as bizarre when asked in 1986. However, in 1990, newspapers were reporting the story of a couple (with no psychiatric illness indicated) having a second baby to supply needed blood for the first-born who was ill. In this context, was the answer "Transfusions" bizarre or not?

Q. What are the disadvantages of having children?
A. First I want to disregard and put aside all those demeanors. I do not like the devil and the devil's advocate.

This would probably be judged a bizarre response by most people.

Medications

Not only may the illness symptoms of the respondent affect the data collected, but medications, often a part of the treatment regimen, may also have a direct bearing on the ability of a patient to respond to a questionnaire or interview schedule. Many seriously ill patients are prescribed one or more medications, either to control acute symptoms or as maintenance at a stable level. However, even when taking medications as prescribed, some patients still experience some illness symptoms, which may be overlaid with medication side effects.

There are numerous books providing helpful descriptions of psychopharmacologic agents. The most basic resource for information on all drugs approved by the United States Food and Drug Administration and manufactured in the country is the *Physician's Desk Reference* (PDR), published annually. Indexed by manufacturer, generic name, and common name, the PDR contains information about indications, contraindications, side effects, suggested dosage, and chemical composition.

There are many types of psychotropic medications. Neuroleptic, or antipsychotic, agents are most often used to treat schizophrenia and other major psychoses; however, they may also be used to treat mania, depression, and severe cases of anxiety (Spiegel & Aebi, 1981). Neuroleptics may be taken by mouth or by periodic intramuscular injection. In acute episodes, medications may be administered intravenously. Many patients receiving neuroleptics also receive a second medication to ameliorate movement disorder side effects. These medications are usually called anti-Parkinsonians or anticholinergics. Tricyclic and tetracyclic antidepressants and monoamine oxidase inhibitors (MAOI) often are used to treat depressive symptoms. Lithium and Tegretol are used to treat bipolar illness. However, there is frequent crossover; people with depression may be given a neuroleptic, while some psychoses (e.g., schizoaffective) may be treated with a neuroleptic plus lithium. Anxiolytics, hypnotics, and anticonvulsant compounds may also be prescribed.

There is great variation in the dose of medication given. Variation may be due to physician or regional prescribing practices; for example, higher doses of neuroleptics are given in the United States than elsewhere (Lewis, Rack, Vaddadi, & Allen, 1980). Acute inpatients are usually given higher doses than are outpatients. However, one should not assume that the size of the dose is related to the severity of the illness or the symptoms. Furthermore, medications are of different potencies, and doses may not be comparable even within general type. There are mathematical formulas that can be used to convert doses of many neuroleptics into chlorpromazine (the first neuroleptic made) equivalent units (Baldessarini, Katz, & Cotton, 1984; Davis, 1974).

Side Effects: In addition to the intended therapeutic action, most medications can produce side effects that may interfere with research participation. Anxiolytics may cause drowsiness and sedation, as may neuroleptics in the first few weeks of use (Spiegel & Aebi, 1981). Drugs known to impair memory include anticholinergics (Yahr & Duvoisin, 1968), antidepressants, and lithium (Marcus, Plasky, & Salzman, 1988). Obviously, such side effects may directly interfere with data collection.

Some side effects can be accommodated within the setting of the interview. Many of the medications (e.g., antipsychotics, antidepressants, and lithium) produce dryness in the mouth and/or bowel irregularities that may make a long interview uncomfortable. Frequent breaks and a dish of hard candies can make a respondent more comfortable. Moreover, some patients taking neuroleptics experience various types of movement disorders. One type of movement side effect is akathesia, in which the individual appears very restless and unable to sit still for long periods of time. These symptoms may be easily misinterpreted by the interviewer as a respondent's impatience with the interview. Again, frequent breaks or a setting where the respondent can move about at will may be desirable.

Course and Chronicity

Course is an illness trait that introduces a time dimension into research. New problems are created when disorders vary in their typical patterns over time. A mental illness may consist of one brief episode that has an acute onset and does not recur. Brief reactive psychosis is one such example.

Other illnesses are characterized by a more chronic course. In medicine, disorders said to be chronic may involve ever-present symptoms, as with spinal cord injury, or they may be cyclical in nature, having periods of acute episodes that alternate with periods of relative medical stability, as might be the case with diabetes. In psychiatry, the usage of "chronic" is similar. Some disorders, such as major depression, are thought to present with relatively consistent symptoms with little intra-individual variation over time. Even so, M. Cohen and Winokur (1988) observe that with one type of endogenous depression, symptoms tend to have a diurnal variation, with maximum severity in the morning. Other disorders, such as schizophrenia, are thought to be more episodic or even cyclical, alternating between decompensation (relapse) and some degree of remission. Bipolar illness (manic-depressive disorder) is especially known for its cycles, in which the patient experiences swings between severe depression and extreme mood elevation or irritability. There may or may not be nonsymptomatic periods between the extremes. Subtypes of the illness are specified by whether the patient is a rapid or slow cycler. According to Coryell and Winokur (1982), research suggests that cyclic patterns stabilize after the initial episodes.

Schizophrenia is a chronic illness having several possible courses. Ciompi (1980) developed an empirical typology of 8 course types, while Huber, Gross, Schuttler, and Linz (1980), developed 12 types. Warner (1985) claims that there are cross-cultural differences in course, with the pattern of progressive deterioration being more characteristic of Western cultures than in Third World cultures.

Research must be sensitive to course issues, especially if one is collecting data from an individual having a cyclical or episodic type of illness. The researcher must be prepared for the eventuality of some psychotic subjects relapsing and being rehospitalized while a study is in progress. Hogarty, Goldberg, Schooler, and Ulrich (1974) found that without treatment, 80% of a sample of patients with schizophrenia relapsed within 24 months. However, in that same study, even patients who were treated with drugs relapsed at the rate of 48% in the same 2-year period. Similarly, persons with bipolar disorder are known to relapse periodically, but less often when taking medication. Thus, one must be sure to know at what point in the cycle the data collection is occurring, because the data will certainly be affected. There are two approaches that may be considered as a compensation for course effects.

One would be to include subjects in the study only at specific points in their cycle, so that cycle becomes a constant. Alternatively, one might include as a variable a measure of the point in each subject's cycle during which data collection occurred.

The cyclical nature of some illnesses may account for low test-retest reliabilities of diagnostic instruments. Symptoms may indeed be different from time to time. The most obvious example is the bipolar patient who may appear manic at one point in time and depressed at another, making diagnosis based only upon present symptoms problematic. Similarly, the respondent may respond to attitudinal questions differently over time, not because of the unreliability of the instrument, but because of real changes in how reality is viewed.

The time dimension inherent in course implies other design issues. When the duration of a disorder is variable, point prevalence studies are particularly susceptible to error (Aneshensel, 1985). Moreover, samples may become biased in favor of the newly diagnosed if a downward course disqualifies part of the subject pool. Changes in treatment plans necessitated by the clinical course of the illness can upset a research design if no provision is made. Modifications may include change in the medication regimen; change in treatment venue from inpatient to outpatient, or vice versa; or changes in geographic location. In addition to modification in the treatment programs, subject mortality may be quite high due to instability in the living conditions common in this population (Sheehan, 1982).

Relapse and chronicity are often intertwined concepts. At one time, chronicity was operationalized as the frequency of rehospitalization, or the number of days spent in hospital. However, with deinstitutionalization, this became an incomplete operationalization (Bachrach, 1976; Goldman, Gattozzi, & Taube, 1981). There has been created a new chronic, the young person who has never been hospitalized and thus would fail the old criteria, but who meets the conceptual criteria of disabling serious illness that is lifelong (Goldman, 1984).

Of particular salience to longitudinal designs involving outpatients will be how the researcher will define and methodologically provide for relapse. Although rehospitalization is appealing as a measure of relapse, rehospitalization is a function not only of patient symptoms, but also of family pressures for commitment, and system variables such as hospital census. Some states provide local systems with financial incentives to reduce rehospitalization (Pharis, 1989), making it more likely for doctors to treat relapses on a outpatient basis. Rehospitalization is a reaction to apparent relapse, and thus only an imperfect operationalization of the concept. It would be preferable to measure directly the behavior of patients, rather than the reaction to their behavior, to estimate relapse. Thus, measures of symptoms or functioning, especially as they deviate from baseline, would be a more desirable approach to relapse.

Given that severe symptoms are likely to intrude in the data collection process, the researcher should consider carefully when during the course of illness any specific study participant should be approached. Individuals in an acute stage of their illness do not make good respondents. Data could be collected through observation or chart review, but probably not through interview or questionnaire. It would be practical to avoid a study design that necessitates the latter techniques during the first days of hospitalization. Direct data collection should wait until stabilization has occurred and/or discharge date nears. This may be possible for cross-sectional psychosocial research designs, but less so for intervention projects dealing specifically with treatment of acutely symptomatic patients.

Whether dealing with inpatients or outpatients, the researcher should consider the routine administration of some indicator(s) of functioning and/or cognitive impairment. Such measures can be used to ascertain the likelihood of collecting valid data, and may also be useful as explanatory or intervening variables in some theoretical models. One easily administered measure for screening severity of psychiatric disturbance is the Global Assessment Scale (GAS) (Endicott, Spitzer, Fleiss, & Cohen, 1976). Used both in research and in clinical settings with satisfactory reliability, a variant of it is recommended in DSM-III-R as Axis V. Unfortunately, the GAS confounds symptoms and functioning as though they were conceptually synonymous, something the researcher may wish to avoid. However, there are alternative choices. Green and Gracely's (1987) analysis of seven brief rating scales (the GAS among them) provides data useful for selecting a specific instrument.

The Mini-Mental Status exam (Folstein, Folstein, & McHugh, 1975) is a widely used instrument for screening cognitive impairment. This brief and easily administered exam can be used prior to interviewing a respondent with suspected dementia or thought disorder. A score below 23 is often considered indicative of cognitive impairment. Others (Holzer, Tischler, Leaf, & Myers, 1984) lower the cutting point to 17 or 18.

RELIABILITY AND VALIDITY OF DATA

The previous discussion implies that data gathered from some mentally ill persons may have problematic reliability and/or validity, not because of weaknesses inherent in the instrument but because of characteristics of the respondents themselves. Spitzer, Endicott, and Robins (1975) suggest that patient variation over time accounts for some of the unreliability in psychiatric diagnosis. Moreover, Bromet, Dunn, Connell, Dew, and Schulberg (1986) reported discouraging results of an 18-month test-retest study of the reliability of diagnosing lifetime major depression. Using the standardized interview, SADS-L applied to the RDC, very low test-retest reliability ($\kappa = .41$) was obtained, even after training yielded inter-rater reliability of .90. The fact that inter-rater reliability was so high, but test-retest reliability so low, indicates that subjects may be providing very inconsistent information from time one to time two.

There are also studies of the validity of patients' self-report of symptoms. Chesney, Larson, Brown, and Bunce (1981) found that psychotic patients generally tended to underreport symptoms when compared to the physician ratings, whereas neurotic patients tended to overreport. Mazure, Nelson, and Price (1986) studied concordant validity of inpatient self-reports of depressive symptoms. Of 12 symptoms, 5 had nonsignificant correlations between self-report and nurses' observations. Among the concordant symptoms, the highest correlation explained less than 50% of the variance, suggesting that patient-supplied symptom data may not be entirely accurate, if one accepts nurses' observations as an adequate standard.

There are few studies of the accuracy of other types of data. In a study of hospitalized women with diagnoses of schizophrenia, McEvoy, Hatcher, Appelbaum, and Abernethy (1983) assessed the accuracy of eight validity questions asked during interviews. Limited to 23 chronically institutionalized subjects, all of whom were taking medication, McEvoy found the overall rate of inaccurate responses to be approximately 32%. Nineteen patients (82%) gave at least one inaccurate answer, while one patient gave six inaccurate answers. Cohen (1988), summarizing the sources of response variability in interviews to determine lifetime prevalence, suggests several variables for the researcher to consider. These include: time since the illness; knowledge base of the respondent; cultural differences; the verbal facility of the respondent; personality traits; motivation of the respondent; redefinitions over time; current mental status; and familiarity with an interview process.

Interlude

The following is an example of problems in data accuracy drawn from a study of 100 outpatients attending two community mental health clinics (Dworkin, Friedman, Telschow, Grant, Moffic, & Sloan, 1990). Sampled patients were previously diagnosed with either a subtype of schizophrenia or a major mood disorder. All had been in treatment for at least 2 years prior to sampling. Thus, all can be said to have a diagnosis of serious, chronic mental illness. Data for selected variables were collected redundantly from multiple independent sources: directly from patients; from clinical charts; and from clinic financial records. Comparison of patient responses with written records provides an estimate of the accuracy that may be expected from mentally ill respondents on questions that require concrete, factual answers. Although there are problems with using archival data (see Chapter 6), for the present purpose the written record comes closest to a gold standard by which to judge the accuracy of patient responses.

When asked: "What is your diagnosis? That is, what does your doctor say is your problem?" only 8% of the responses matched exactly the diagnosis (down to the subtype) recorded in the clinical chart. More broadly interpreted, 27% of the patients named the appropriate general diagnostic category that contained their specific diagnosis entered into the chart. These responses included those that were generally correct, but inaccurate in detail (e.g., a patient diagnosed with paranoid schizophrenia reported that his diagnosis was "hypertensive schizophrenia"). Approximately 18% gave a vague response acknowledging a mental illness (e.g., "nervous breakdown," "crazy") or emotional distress (e.g., "insomnia"). The remaining 53% either did not reply, or said they were not ill, or gave a medical illness (e.g., "liver problem") instead. Generally, patients with a diagnosis of a mood disorder more often named a diagnosis compatible with their chart than did patients with a diagnosis of schizophrenia.

Patients were also asked six questions regarding the types of treatment they were currently receiving (i.e., talking with caseworker; seeing the psychiatrist; attending medication group; day treatment; injections by the nurse; going to activity groups) in a fixed choice format (yes or no). Approximately 37% of the patients gave responses to the six questions that were in agreement with their clinical chart. Another 37% gave responses with one discrepancy. Twenty-six percent of the patients gave responses that contained two or more contradictions with the chart. No one disagreed with the chart on all six. In addition, patients were asked for certain numerical information that could be compared against written records: frequency of clinic visits; fees paid on the last visit; and length of time in treatment at the clinic. The correlation of each estimate with the record was: $r = .44$ ($p < .05$); $r = .13$ ($p > .05$); and $r = .48$ ($p < .05$), respectively. Although correlations of .40 may be satisfactory for model testing, they are low values as measures of validity. Hypothesizing that the low associations may be due to poor patient functioning, the rating on the Global Assessment Scale made at the time of each interview and the absolute differences between patient estimates and the written record were correlated. It would be desirable to state that accuracy of information is directly and closely related to the level of patient functioning. Unfortunately, that relationship was inconsistently found and is probably more complex than a simple straight-line function. Additional analysis suggests that for low functioning patients, there may be a moderate relationship between patient functioning and data accuracy; but for higher functioning patients, there was no such relationship. However, this pattern was also unstable. Thus, the relationship between accuracy of information and level of patient functioning remains unclear.

Low levels of accuracy suggest that the patient may not be the best source of certain types of information. This is especially true when studying children. When available, patient-supplied data should be confirmed from other sources. However, there are some data that can be obtained only from the patient. These include attitudinal data, and reports of behavior neither witnessed by a designated informant nor subject to routine record keeping. Whatever the data content may be, the researcher must be mindful that a patient's responses may reflect a definition of the situation experienced by the respondent, but which is not necessarily shared by others nor confirmable from other sources of information.

PROXY INTERVIEWS

It is foreseeable that some individuals sampled for interviews or questionnaires may be unable to respond meaningfully due to the intensity of experienced symptoms and/or the side effects of medication. In this situation, the researcher may consider interviewing the significant other(s) about the ill individual. Using a significant other, usually a member of the immediate family, to supply a medical history and other information is routinely done in clinical practice (Davidson & Davidson, 1983).

Anthropologists and sociologists doing fieldwork are accustomed to the technique of informant interviewing. In that context informants supply information about a culture or group to which they belong, rather than supply detailed information about a specific individual who is unable to answer for himself or herself. In the latter case, the informant is being a proxy for the true subject of the investigation, with the assumption made that the information given by the proxy will be equivalent to the information that would be given by the subject if the latter were able to supply the information. Although the technique is not commonly discussed in the social and behavioral science methodological literature, there is precedence for using the technique. Household surveys, such as those done by the United States Census and National Opinion Research Center, typically interview one adult who supplies information about the head of household and others in the family.

Methodological research on using proxy interviews for the study of mental illness has focused upon studies of the occurrence of disorders, particularly bipolar illness, in families. In particular, there have been many studies comparing the data obtained from family history techniques (i.e., interviewing patients and one or two informants about all family members) and family study techniques (i.e., interviewing all family members about themselves). Andreasen, Rice, Endicott, Reich, and Coryell (1986); Andreasen, Endicott, Spitzer, and Winokur (1977); and Mendlewicz, Fleiss, Cataldo, and Rainer (1975) strongly suggest that proxy interviewing underestimates the extent of illness in a family, compared to estimates obtained through interviewing each family member. Furthermore, Thompson, Orvaschel, Prusoff, and Kidd (1982) found that using proxies in a family history method yielded diagnoses with high specificity, but lower sensitivity, and that accuracy was greater for the more serious diagnoses than the less serious.

In addition to studies of diagnosis using family history/family study methodologies, the accuracy of proxy data has been studied with regard to other variables. Proxy assessment of patient outcome has been one area that has produced inconsistent results. Vestre and Zimmerman's (1969) findings suggest that relatives' ratings are as good as those of nurses in the rating of psychiatric symptoms and behavior. However, Garfield, Prager, and Bergin (1971) reported low correlations among patient's, therapist's, and supervisor's assessment of patient progress. On that basis, Garfield, Prager, and Bergin (1974) argue that disagreements between data sources will be quite common. Others (see Davidson & Davidson, 1983) are more optimistic in the use of proxies. Still another focus is typified by Yager, Grant, Sweetwood, and Gerst (1981), who compared couples on the Holmes and Rahe (1967) Schedule of Recent Experiences and found that both patient and nonpatient couples had low agreement as measured by Cohen's kappas (.35 and .39, respectively), with patient pairs having only slightly lower agreements.

There is also controversy over how much data quality is improved by the use of a proxy, and how many proxies are optimal. Although Thompson et al. (1982) argue that multiple informants do not improve data quality due to correlated error, others (Andreasen et al., 1977; Gershon & Guroff, 1984; Mendlewicz et al., 1975) found that accuracy increases with the number of proxies interviewed. Schless and Mendels (1978), in a series of studies on proxy assessment of life stressors, estimated that a third party, used as an extra validity check, added 29% new information over that gathered by the proxy's interview added to the subject's interview. However, Gershon and Guroff suggest that for an estimation of detailed diagnosis, four informants are needed to produce acceptable concordance with the personal interview. Because of the expense and logistical problems of obtaining so many interviews, it is to be hoped that a smaller quantity of detailed information than that required to make a diagnosis may be obtained accurately from fewer informants. Andreasen et al. (1986) suggest that data quality improves by reducing the detail of the information requested by using broad, but well-specified definitions, which implies that carefully conceptualized and composed instruments may obviate the need for multiple proxies.

When selecting proxies one must consider the relationship of the proxy to the subject. Thompson et al. (1982) found more accurate data were obtained from spouses and offspring than from parents and siblings, a factor that might be considered when selecting a proxy. Furthermore, any proxy will have access to only certain kinds of information. Easily hidden behaviors may not be within the proxy's ability to disclose. Furthermore, proxies cannot be expected to give valid information with regard to the subject's attitudes, beliefs, and perceptions. Hence, Strupp and Hadley (1977) suggest using proxies for information about social functioning, but not for the subject's subjective states. However, even with this conservative approach, there are issues of bias raised that must be considered.

The availability of an appropriate individual to give a proxy interview may itself have a biasing effect, since mentally ill people with significant others nearby may be different than those whose families are either geographically or socially distant (Clausen, 1972). This may be even more true today than when Clausen made that observation. With more patients living outside institutions, differential pressures on families for withdrawal from their kin with psychiatric illness may produce greater opportunity for bias than previously.

Furthermore, the reports of family are likely to be emotionally laden; and may include defensiveness and projection (Davidson & Davidson, 1983); and may reflect their own concerns about the illness, which are often different from that of the patients (Kreisman & Joy, 1975; Sappington & Michaux, 1975; Targum, Dibble, Davenport, & Gershon, 1981). Although this difference may be an important datum, care should be taken to avoid the cross-contamination of proxy and target. Moreover, since some illnesses have a heavy familial component, a proxy could exhibit some level of mental disturbance, and this could have a biasing effect. According to a review by Cohen (1988), depressed mothers tend to overestimate emotional problems in their children. In another review, A. Ross (1978) suggests that parents tend to be more positive in their evaluation of treatment outcomes than do outside observers.

Data collection costs will be escalated just in the selecting and locating of an appropriate proxy. If the proxy is used in addition to the subject, costs will increase further, especially if more than one proxy per subject is used.

If proxies are to be used, one might reconsider the choice of measurements. There are versions of some instruments especially prepared to be administered to significant others. The Katz Adjustment Scale–Relative's Form (Katz & Lyerly, 1963) is a widely used proxy instrument for social and community functioning. The Family History–Research Diagnostic Criteria (Endicott, Andreasen, & Spitzer, 1975) is a proxy instrument for diagnosis.

If one plans to collect proxy data from others (e.g., family, friends, employer, and so on) consent from the target must be obtained first. To do otherwise would reveal facts about the subject (e.g., that he or she is a patient) that can be an invasion of privacy and can put the patient at risk (Hays, 1975). However, at least one team (Weissman & Bothwell, 1976) reported subjects being reluctant to have even their spouses interviewed.

Of course when multiple sources are used, one risks obtaining information that is blatantly contradictory. How is consensus between data sources to be reached? It cannot be assumed that one data source is a priori preferred over another. In the absence of gold standards, the researcher needs to generate strategies to referee differences. Where contradictions exist over matters of fact, differences may be resolved by using the most logically consistent information available. Alternatively, one may need another proxy or need to have another source of information available, such as the clinical chart, to arbitrate the difference. Where the contradictions flow from subjective perceptions or judgments, perhaps consensus should not be attempted; rather, each person's perception may be included as a separate variable, conceptually distinct from the others.

Thus, proxies either may be used exclusively or may be one of several sources of information used along with subject interviews, clinical chart review, and institutional statistics in a multimethod design. The principle of the multimethod approach for triangulation (Campbell & Fiske, 1959) is well accepted, although not always practiced in the social sciences. However, when researching the mentally ill, multimethod approaches often become a matter of necessity rather than an abstract principle.

ETHICAL ISSUES

Informed Consent

Ethical concerns in research on human subjects (i.e., knowledge, volunteerism, confidentiality, cost/benefit ratio) all balance upon informed consent. The National Commission for the Protection of Human Subjects of Biomedical and Behavioral Research (1978) considers the mentally ill a population needing special protection much like the protection awarded to children and prisoners. The concern has been focused upon the institutionalized, an easily manipulated captive research population (Barber, 1980), where exploitative research has been done that was not germane to the condition of the patient (National Commission, 1978). The issues are generalizable to the deinstitutionalized as well. Of special concern is the patient's ability to give consent that is truly informed and consensual when cognitive ability is compromised due to illness, and autonomy is compromised due to hospitalization or involvement in other treatment contexts. Since the mentally ill may be more vulnerable to coercion and they may not understand the consequences of the research and hence may not be fully informed (Ashely, 1975), the validity of their consent can be problematic.

Federal guidelines assume that the well-written consent form can be understood by the average person (Rosoff, 1981), and that statements of possible benefits, either in terms of personal gain or a greater good, are understood and weighed against possible harm before the patient accedes. However, this is an overly optimistic view. Lidz, Meisel, Zerubavel, Carter, Sestak, and Roth (1984) reported that patients typically had incomplete or wrong understanding of consent. Irwin, Lovitz, Marder, Mintz, Winslade, VanPutten, and Mills (1985) found that acutely psychotic patients were able to read informed consents and reported understanding the material. However, objective measures of understanding did not confirm the patients' self-reports. Furthermore, the severity of the thought disorder seemed to be related to the ability to understand the consent (Irwin et al.). Education has also been consistently found to be a predictor of understanding (Lidz et al., 1984; Taub, 1986). In addition, what understanding patients did acquire came over time (Lidz et al.). Taub found that results were best when informed consent was given multiple times throughout a study.

Evidence has been found of coercive effects outside the traditional mental hospital. Abrams (1988) points out that, when approached by a medical authority figure, demented elderly in nursing homes may consent to research for fear that their medical treatment will be prejudiced. Lidz et al. found that patients often were pressured by other patients to consent.

How, then, is capability to give informed consent to be determined? Since the definition of mental illness is so broad and covers such a wide spectrum of conditions, having a diagnosable mental illness is not grounds for disqualifying consent. Moreover, competence/incompetence cannot be used as a guideline either. Incompetence is a legal concept and requires court adjudication initiated by some interested party. An individual could be disassociated from reality, and involuntarily hospitalized, and still be legally competent (Rosoff, 1981). From a practical and ethical viewpoint, it may be impossible to obtained valid informed consent from someone, even if he or she has never been judicially determined incompetent. Thus legal competence, although a necessary condition for consent capability, is not sufficient. Furthermore, a patient may be capable of giving consent on one day, but not on another (Annas, Glantz, & Katz, 1977). Thus, the researcher needs some measurable standard by which to judge the prospective research subject's ability to understand consent on the day it is given. This standard should go beyond legal status and should be independent of diagnosis.

There are basic differences between informed consent for treatment and for research in terms of the risk/benefit ratio. In treatment, there is putative benefit for the patient along with some medically acknowledged risk. However, there is often no personal benefit to the research subject. Research ethicists such as Annas et al. make the distinction between therapeutic and nontherapeutic research, and suggest different levels of consent for each.

Although most psychosocial research is of minimal risk, there are potential dangers that must be acknowledged even if the study only involves questionnaires. There is the expenditure of time and effort. Some patients may enjoy the attention received during an interview; however, disclosures of personal information could raise fears that may be stressful for a mentally ill respondent, exposing the person to additional psychological risk. Since mental illness is a stigmatized condition, participation in a study known to be about mental illness may pose social and economic risk for the participant.

Risks are multiplied when experimental designs are used (especially with placebo controls) or when emotionally invasive procedures are indicated. If the research is multidisciplinary, the social scientist may be working in projects with research interventions and/or medical procedures. Even drawing blood and collecting urine specimens carry minor risks that must be minimized by the researcher and understood by the patient.

Moreover, although most people are familiar with receiving medical care for which they give consent, research is usually a concept not clearly understood. Lidz et al. found that patients in psychiatric research could not clearly distinguish between the therapeutic goals and nontherapeutic goals, and so could not appreciate the costs of participation in the research.

The use of proxy consent is a controversial alternative to patient consent. The National Commission for the Protection of Human Subjects (1978) and Taub (1986) suggest the possibility of consent by proxy or guardian. Hays (1975) recommends that a guardian sign for the acutely psychotic patient, while Ashely (1975) recommends the practice with any mentally ill person. The research of Warren, Sobal, Tenney, Hoopes, Damron, Levenson, DeForge, and Muncie (1986) suggests that proxies do not always act in accordance to their perceptions of their charge's wishes. Annas and Glanz (1986) also see the practice as questionable.

In summary, suggestions for informed consent include the following. Take a more protective stance toward the rights of the mentally ill than would ordinarily be the case. Give special attention to obtaining informed consent. The process should be more than an empty ritual. Because of possible coercive effects, avoid having a caregiver administer the informed consent. Consent should be given in individual sessions one-on-one. This will avoid peer pressure, both for and against participation. Write the consent form at an easy reading level and in concrete language. Screen respondents for comprehension, not just recall. Consider consent to be an ongoing process. Multiple administrations will give a patient with a cyclical illness the opportunity to reconsider. It will also improve retention and understanding of the information. Do not rely upon legal competency to determine consent capability. Include criteria that are measurable. Avoid study designs that necessitate initial enrollment of actively psychotic patients since their ability to give consent is most questionable. Cooperation of the family is often desirable for achieving patient compliance and cooperation; however, this is appropriate only where confidentiality will not be compromised and when the patient gives his or her consent. Consider the appropriateness of proxy consent by parents or guardians to augment patient consent or assent.

Control Groups

In addition to informed consent, the experimental research design that requires either placebo or no treatment control groups nearly always raises ethical questions. To deny a group of patients access to treatment is counter to the values of most caregivers; it may generate political controversy and it may violate a researcher's humanitarian values.

The design that specifies an untreated control is open to greatest criticism. Where there is a known efficacious treatment, withholding treatment is difficult to justify ethically. Untreated controls are acceptable only when there is no standard treatment. Even when the control consists of the standard treatment, many research protocols include a provision for referral of subjects to the more efficacious treatment discovered after the conclusion of the data collection. Although this will increase research costs, the practice may be ethically necessary and politically astute.

INTERVIEWER SELECTION

Although some instruments are explicitly designed for the layperson, and others are designed for use by mental health workers, Klerman (1985) cites unresolved professional conflicts over the credentials of interviewers. Regarding instruments designed for nonclinician interviewers, current work indicates that clinician-nonclinician interview differences may be minimal. Helzer et al. (1981) report that the RDI administered by psychiatrists have somewhat higher sensitivity, but interviews done by nonpsychiatrists have higher specificity. Likewise Helzer, Spitznagel, and McEvoy (1987) found minor clinician-nonclinician differences when using the DIS with an inpatient population. Furthermore, predictive validity was quite similar for both types of interviewers in a community sample.

However, results were different when Anthony, Folstein, Romanoski, Von Korff, Nestadt, Chahal, Merchant, Brown, Shapiro, Kramer, and Gruenberg (1985) compared the results of the DIS administered by nonpsychiatrists with a clinical reappraisal administered by psychiatrists using the Present State Examination protocol. They found rather low agreement between the two types of interviews. It is unclear whether the low agreement is due to different types of interviewers or to different interview protocols, or to changes in the respondents during the intervening time.

Thus, decisions about the interviewer and instruments to be used must necessarily be closely interrelated. The ability of an instrument to obtain valid and reliable research data, while minimizing interviewer costs by using nonclinicians, may be an important factor in the choice of diagnostic instrument.

However, selection of an instrument is only one factor that will influence one's choice of data gatherer. There are occasions when an interviewing psychiatrist may be reactive. People who have "fought the mental illness wars" may become cynical and suspicious of caregivers in an interviewing situation. Conversely, if the reporting of subjective experience is important in the interview, the caregiver may be better able to establish empathic rapport.

If the researcher decides to hire data collectors drawn from a general pool of social science interviewers, practical problems arise. Whereas it requires only routine hiring and training procedures to acquire interviewers for a general survey, difficulties should be anticipated when the subjects are mentally ill. Attitudes of the general population toward mentally ill persons tend to be negative (Link & Cullen, 1986; Rabkin, 1980), with the public often believing mentally ill people to be dangerous, unpredictable, and intimidating. Although interviewers trained in the social sciences and/or health professions may have greater understanding of and interest in persons with a mental illness, there still exists the possibility of difficulty in finding an adequate pool of interviewer candidates.

A study of interviewer preferences and experience (Dworkin, 1989b) suggests that interviewing mentally ill persons is not a desirable prospect for most potential interviewers. Out of 18 interviewing targets presented, interviewing the mentally ill ranked next to the last. Interviewing convicted felons, cancer patients, and AIDS patients are all preferred. Those who report experience interviewing the mentally ill tend to have somewhat higher preference scores than those with no such experience. Interviewers with social work backgrounds have a slightly stronger preference for interviewing mentally ill subjects, compared with people coming from other majors (Dworkin & Dworkin, 1989). However, there is no evidence to suggest that basic social science college majors are inappropriate candidates for recruitment. Since they are a ready labor supply for social science research, they remain a good source of interviewers.

Although one cannot conclude from the Dworkin and Dworkin (1989) study that the quality of interviews would be impacted, one should anticipate that quality could be adversely affected. When interviewers expect difficulty in obtaining responses, the nonresponse rates increase

(Singer, Frankel, & Glassman, 1983) and target behaviors are underreported (Bradburn & Sudman, 1979). Moreover, respondents perceived as intimidating may cause the interviewer to record in a biased or incorrect manner (Hyman, 1954). Respondent-interviewer interaction effects have been noted in the recording of alcohol consumption (Cosper, 1969; Mulford & Miller, 1951) and in responses to psychological symptom scales (Cleary, Mechanic, & Weiss, 1981).

When studying mentally ill persons, one would expect to encounter similar problems: inappropriate behavior or statements by interviewers that may alienate respondents; reticence of interviewers to probe for fear of inducing an outburst; misinterpretation of respondents' statements by interviewers; and shortened or incomplete interviews. These factors should become important issues during training and supervision.

Interviewing site is another aspect of the research protocol that must be considered. Interviewers prefer to work with mentally ill respondents in environments that maximize control and cooperation (Dworkin & Dworkin, 1989). Least-favored sites include unannounced door-to-door interviews, telephone interviews, and interviews conducted in a public place. More-favored locales include special interviewing offices and treatment centers. Unfortunately, a special interviewing site may be unavailable or too expensive. Furthermore, access to clinical environments may be problematic and even methodologically inappropriate for some studies, given the implied a priori limitations of populations in treatment. Nevertheless, the researcher should consider protected sites when they are methodologically appropriate. Even if most favored environments are unavailable, the researcher should avoid expecting interviewers to arrive unannounced at a respondent's doorstep. To make interviewing more desirable work, the researcher may have to be prepared to offer higher wages, greater benefits, or more pleasant working conditions in order to attract appropriate personnel.

The researcher should consider spending a longer time in interviewer training than would ordinarily be spent if a general population were to be studied. Of course, training for the specific interview protocol must be thorough. But in addition, a part of the training should focus upon attitudes about mental illness as well as special situations and behaviors likely to be encountered by the interviewer. Gibbon, McDonald-Scott, and Endicott (1981) suggest a training procedure that includes case vignettes, videotaped interviews done by experienced interviewers, practice interviews, and continued monitoring. Although specifically developed for diagnostic interviewing for research, Gibbon et al.'s training protocol could be usefully adapted for any type of interviewing. In particular, videotapes of people exhibiting a variety of symptoms likely to be encountered, and demonstrations of how one might deal with those symptoms in an interview situation, would be a necessary orientation for the interviewer inexperienced with mental illness. Training should be directed not only to appropriate interviewing behavior, but also to desensitizing the novice to the mystique of mental illness and the threat that it holds for many.

6

Alternative Data Sources

Data about the mentally ill may be obtained through means other than directly from interviews or questionnaires administered to the target respondent. This chapter will discuss some of these alternatives: the clinical chart, institutional data, and large data banks. Because the clinical chart may be unfamiliar to many researchers inexperienced in the medical arena, the topic will be discussed first, in considerable detail.

CLINICAL CHARTS

Patient records (clinical charts) are an alternative data source that is attractive to many researchers. They have been a mainstay for research not only in the area of mental illness (Smith, Sjoberg, & Phillips, 1969), but also in other medically oriented research. As such, many of the techniques, problems, and benefits of using charts are common to archival research on a variety of patient populations.

The clinical chart is the official record of patient history and progress and is considered an essential function in the provision of health care (Waters & Murphy, 1979). Information contained within the psychiatric record generally consists of four major types (Siegel & Fischer, 1981a): administrative (e.g., identification, financial, social, and legal data); assessments (e.g., history, mental status exams, and psychological testing); plans (e.g., treatment plans, recommendations, and orders); documentation of care (e.g., medical treatment and other services given, patient progress, case conferences, and discharge summaries). Its purpose is to provide a current and ongoing record of what is done for an individual patient while also serving as a memory device for the caregivers. Hence, the record is a dynamic, longitudinal document.

There are usually special entries made and forms completed when the record is first opened upon admission to the facility. This information commonly includes the basic socio-demographic information; financial data; patient history, often in terms of reports sent by previous caregivers; and an initial assessment. Special information is also entered when the record is closed. This may include a detailed open-ended discharge summary and/or a standardized discharge form. Between admission and discharge there should be a running record that includes notes documenting treatment (including medications prescribed), visits, tests, transfers, and telephone calls. In the case of long-term treatment, there may also be periodic updates of information previously gathered. The patient record may be the responsibility of a team of staff having varying roles in the treatment of the patient. Some information, such as financial forms, may be filled out by a clerk or financial secretary. Other information may be entered by social workers, nurses, psychologists, and psychiatrists. Occupational, art, and other specialized therapists may also contribute. Sometimes one person, such as a caseworker, carries the overall responsibility for chart completion, while the psychiatrist has the responsibility for medically specific information.

Charts contain information in two formats. Information may be supplied on standard forms (i.e., standard in that institution or practice). A hospital will probably have standard intake forms and/or discharge forms in which certain information is recorded in structured, forced choice, or short answer formats, similar in style to a questionnaire. These forms generally are meant to supply very basic socio-demographic and background information and sometimes includes a diagnostic code.

Charts also usually contain open-ended sections, sometimes called progress notes. The unstructured, open-ended entries may contain summaries of psychotherapy sessions or recommendations made during supportive therapy. Many clinicians utilize an approach known as Problem Oriented Medical Record (POMR). Developed by Weed (1971), the approach organizes record keeping around problems that have been enumerated for each patient. For each problem, the progress notes ought to contain several elements. Over time, these elements have been reduced to four, known by the acronym, SOAP: Subjective data (patient symptoms), Objective data (physical findings and laboratory tests), Assessment (interpretations relative to the specific problem), and Plan (treatment recommendations). Regardless of whether they adhere to a SOAP format, progress notes remain open-ended; the length and content will vary considerably by institution and by the style of individual clinicians. The open-ended and closed-ended formats each have their own special problems and strengths as well as shared problems and limitations.

Advantages of Chart Data

Charts, once accessed, offer many methodological and logistical advantages. Information from charts can be obtained quickly and cheaply, compared to that obtained through interviewing. Although coders need to be well trained and supervised, the level of expertise needed is probably less than that needed by interviewers.

Charts contain information gathered from a variety of sources and do not depend wholly upon the ability of patients to provide information at a specific time. However, it must be understood that, although gathered from different sources (e.g., patient, patient's family, records from other treatment facilities, results of psychological testing, clinical interviews, and so on), this information is filtered through the interpretations of the clinician keeping the record.

Since the chart provides longitudinal data, it is possible to do historical prospective studies without the delays caused by real-time longitudinal work. Siegel and Fischer (1981a) suggest that because of the availability of large numbers of charts, they are useful to study traits of patients assigned to various treatments and also to study the efficacy of those treatments (given nonrandom assignment in a quasi-experimental design).

Limitations of Chart Data

The most crucial understanding the researcher must have about the clinical chart is that the chart does not exist for the purpose of accumulating research data. Rather, the chart serves a range of needs, of which research usually has a low(est) priority. The function of the clinical record is the recording and interpretation of patient history and behavior, both positive and negative, and the course of prescribed treatments, in an effort to prompt the memory of the treatment staff and to provide for continuity in treatment and reduction of redundant efforts. Today charts are not merely records of patient history and progress; they are also bureaucratic, legal, and financial records. Several different interested parties influence the content of records. Salient parties include the insurance industry, federal and state governments, and the Joint Commission on Accreditation. Because records are neither designed by researchers nor exist for the exclusive use of researchers, there will be problems in their use as a research tool.

Any discussion of using clinical charts must begin with the recognition that many have reservations about the reliability and validity of data entered into medical records (Fessel & Van Brunt, 1972). Murnaghan and White (1971) succinctly summarize the basic problem with charts: "As every physician knows, the typical medical record is disorganized, illegible, incomplete or not to be found in the first place" (p. 825). Ten years later Esrov (1981) and Siegel and Fischer (1981a) made essentially the same observations. Sadly, the situation still has not changed significantly, even with the advent of computerization of records in many locales. The researcher needs to assess the general quality of the records first, and then, if they are adequate, tailor data collection techniques so that high quality data will be collected and the dross will be discarded.

Access

Researchers from outside the service facility may have difficulty obtaining initial access. Permission to review records is usually granted on the organizational level from a gatekeeper or regulating committee. If the gatekeeper refuses access, the entire site is lost to the researcher. However, once access is granted, the researcher need not be concerned with response rate on the level of the individual patient. Some agencies prefer that patients sign a general release of information for research purposes when their charts are initially opened, just as they may be asked to sign release of information to other caregivers within the system. Once a general release is signed, consent is usually not required for each specific research use. However, one should consult the appropriate Institutional Review Board for local policy. Sieber (1991) discusses alternatives in detail.

Disorganization

Charts are typically disorganized. Although they may be physically partitioned into several sections, there will be enormous variation in sequencing and format. Although an agency may mandate the use of specific forms, there still may be variation within a specific facility as to where certain information is located in the chart, or if those forms are even used. This slows the coder who must search for out-of-sequence information that may ultimately be overlooked because of its location.

Comparability

There will be inconsistencies over time and place in the style of the chart and/or the standard forms used, reflecting changes in system policy and personnel. Incompatibility commonly occurs with inter-organizational research (Esrov, 1981). Canfield, Clarkin, Coyne, and Grob (1986) suggest that even with comparable forms, data reliability may be a significant problem across institutions. In particular, when data are to be found in several different locations within the charts, coders may use different sources for their ratings and thereby decrease reliability.

Another comparability issue is raised with structured forms. Information that was gathered in unstructured ways may be entered onto standard structured forms. This may produce data that are unreliable, in much the way that DSM-III-R diagnoses may be unreliable if obtained using nonstandardized clinical interviews.

Legibility

Writing is sometimes illegible. Entries in clinical charts tend to confirm the cultural stereotype that physicians' handwriting is unreadable. A study by Siegel and Fischer (1981c), however, found fewer legibility problems than others have suggested. They found that records were generally readable, although the unstructured sections, such as progress notes, were less so. They also found that private institutions tended to have entries typed more often than did state institutions, thus producing records that tended to be more readable.

Sampling

When using clinical charts as the data source, the working population necessarily is defined as cases in treatment at that specific locale(s). There are fundamental biases inherent in sampling cases under treatment. Data cannot be collected on persons who might be considered ill but have not entered treatment. And unless there is access to inactive records, data will not be collected from patients who have dropped out of treatment. Thus, if the records are used for a retrospective study of treatment efficacy, the archive may contain only those patients who are engaged in active treatment, and not those who have dropped out perhaps because of treatment inefficacy.

Using chart data in some respects simplifies sampling procedures. One may sample charts directly from file cabinets, by beginning at a random starting point and then selecting every nth chart until the necessary number of cases is drawn. With this method there is the danger of omitting charts that have been placed elsewhere for special purposes. It is not recommended that the researcher draw charts by taking one every nth inch, since this will bias the sample toward those patients having the thickest charts. The sample would then contain patients who have been under treatment longer than others, who are seen more often, and/or who are sicker. Sometimes the files of patients in most frequent contact with a clinic are kept in the office of a caseworker for that person's convenience. Thus, sampling only from a central filing room may systematically miss the most frequent users of the facility.

Lists of the treatment population for drawing samples are frequently obtainable from clinic or hospital personnel. Because of the low cost of such data collection, larger samples than are necessary are sometimes used. Even samples containing entire populations with thousands of charts are not too uncommon.

Missing Charts

Murnaghan and White (1971) point out that charts sometimes cannot be found. In a large chart review study (Adams, Dworkin, & Knox, 1985) clinical charts ($n = 1,752$) were coded and then were to be used one year later for a follow-up. The study was done in a closed system where charts physically followed patients to one of six treatment facilities; if a case became inactive, the chart was to be sent to a central medical records storage library. Of the original 1,752 charts coded, 93.3% were relocated the next year by searching each of the seven locations. To a longitudinal survey researcher a nonresponse rate of less than 7% over one year sounds excellent. However, in a system where all records are to remain accessible, the histories of 116 people were lost both to clinicians and to researchers. These records could have been merely misfiled, or names may have been changed, or patient case numbers may have been miscopied by staff. Conversely, it is possible for an individual to be counted twice by having more than one record opened, especially if the patient has had multiple admissions.

Missing Data

Standard forms within charts often have information noticeably missing. The extent of the incompleteness, its source, and its implications vary with the format of the relevant section of the chart. Since the medical record is the principal source of information used in assessing quality of care (Koran, 1975), it may be that the most complete parts of a chart will be those emphasized by external review committees for their audits (Casper, 1987). There is some evidence to suggest that records in state and Veterans Affairs facilities are more complete than those in private institutions (Siegel & Fischer, 1981b).

One reason for incompleteness is that some patients may have been treated by several different caregivers, either sequentially or simultaneously. In particular, patients with serious illness experience a variety of caregivers over the years. Unless these different clinicians are aware of one another so that records can follow the patient, any one chart will be incomplete. It is not known whether there are biases introduced due to different reasons for failure of the records to follow the patient. It should be noted that a patient may choose not to give permission for a record to be released to subsequent clinicians.

Missing data may also be due to incompleteness of record keeping at the treatment site being studied. Mental health professionals often place a low value upon doing paperwork (Casper, 1987), often believing that it does not contribute to quality patient care. With a low priority placed upon such work, completion of required forms may be delayed or entirely omitted. Perlman, Schwartz, Paris, Thornton, Smith, and Weber (1982) studied the completeness of chart information required by Medicaid, at 29 free-standing psychiatric clinics and 6 hospital psychiatric outpatient clinics in New York, and concluded that incomplete information was the norm rather than the exception. Moreover, they found that the hospital clinics contained significantly more of the mandated information than did the free-standing clinics. Affiliation with medical schools had no impact, nor did the amount of Medicaid payments. Patient's sex did not impact the completeness of information. However, ethnicity did; compared to records of white and black patients, the medical records of Hispanic patients were significantly less complete, possibly due to language problems. Records were more complete for patients with psychosis, neuroses, and personality disorders than for patients with substance-abuse diagnoses. Finally, Perlman's team found that completeness varied by the interaction of the discipline of the record keeper and the facility type. In the free-standing clinics, psychiatrists kept more complete records. However, in the hospital clinics, psychiatrists scored lower in completeness than did other professionals. Social workers and psychologists tended to produce more complete records than did others.

Biases introduced by missing data in charts can be subtle and difficult to identify (Dworkin, 1987). Missing chart data are not necessarily due to nonresponse on the part of the unit of observation (i.e., the patient). Thus, searching for bias by comparing patients having complete data with those having missing data will overlook characteristics of the record keeper that may impact both record completeness and the variables under study. This may be particularly salient given that cases are often assigned differentially to staff (Baekeland & Lundwall, 1975).

Studies of missing chart data (Dworkin, 1987; Perlman et al., 1982) strongly suggest that the missing-at-random assumption may be seriously violated and should not be made automatically when chart data are involved. In particular, if one can infer the clinician's attitude toward the patient by the completeness of the medical record, as Perlman et al. suggest, then it is probable that the data are not randomly omitted. A study using patient variables that are affected by the clinician (such as retention in treatment or treatment efficacy) will be seriously biased by missing data problems (Dworkin, 1987).

Finally, it must be remembered that incomplete data are most obvious when a structured form is examined; some items are left blank. When open-ended notes are coded, one can never know what is missing. If something is *not* present in the notes the researcher cannot judge if it did not happen, or if the record was incompletely written.

Information Accuracy and Consistency

In addition to being incomplete, data can also be incorrect. Although, little research has been done on the sources of data inaccuracy in psychiatric records, informational mistakes may be substantial. Esrov (1981), Murnaghan and White (1971), and Gehlbach (1979) all point to the problems of inaccuracy in data contained in medical records. Some errors can be identified because they are logically inconsistent. These can be recognized without any specialized knowledge of the patient. The chart of a 15-year-old child who has 16 years of formal education clearly contains an error. Not only is such an error easily recognized, it may also be correctable if coders have been trained to cross-check doubtful, contradictory, or inconsistent information against other sources of information within the record. Other errors may consist of incorrectly entered neuropsychological test scores, laboratory values, or medication doses. Although identification of this type of error may require psychological or medical expertise, sometimes these errors make themselves known as outlyers in frequency distributions. Other factual inaccuracies may be difficult or impossible to identify without detailed knowledge of the individual obtained elsewhere.

Some inaccuracies or contradictions may be due to the same methodological problems that haunt questionnaire design. If structured forms are developed that violate principles of sound instrument construction, the quality of chart information will suffer. For example, if forms are created with long checklists, the record keeper may respond within a response set, identical to the yea-saying effect found in some questionnaires.

Interlude

A study of the effect of changes in the fee schedule upon outpatient treatment illustrates how information gathered for different reasons and recorded in different chart locations may be inconsistent. As part of a revised fee policy in a large agency, all patients were to have new financial statement forms completed. Patients were newly required to provide written documentation of their personal and family incomes to minimize underestimation of financial resources.

As part of the study, patients' gross annual income data were coded from two different sources in the clinical charts of 108 outpatients at two different treatment facilities. Prior to the change, income was coded from an initial contact form that was filled out by either the caseworker or the clerical staff. This was a general purpose form with income only a minor item. As part of the implementation of the policy change, gross income was also recorded by the facilities' billing clerk on a new financial data form. The latter form was completed with staff and patient both aware that this could raise the fees paid by the client.

Although it was expected that both income figures would be underestimates, it was anticipated that the newer form would yield higher incomes because of the documentation required. Reported gross income was compared for those patients who had both new and old forms completed in the chart and no reported change in employment status. When the income data were compared from the two different sources, it was found that the mean gross income reported on the new form was nearly $2,400 *lower* than previously reported ($t = 2.85$; $df = 57$; $p = .006$). During interviews, clerks admitted that they were aware that the new form "really mattered"; that they did not always ask for the required documentation; and that clinic staff were concerned that patients would drop out of treatment if they were forced to pay for services. It would appear that the income estimates that had real consequences were greatly underestimated as staff attempted to protect their patients/clients.

Selective Reporting

In addition to missing data, it has been observed that records are otherwise incomplete (Siegel & Fischer, 1981a), but in less easily identifiable ways. Open-ended entries, in particular, may omit critical observations or episodes. Even the occurrence of dramatic events may go unrecorded in the clinical chart. Lion, Snyder, and Merrill (1981) document that in one hospital only about 18.3% of violent incidents were recorded. Taylor (1986) similarly observed the underreporting of violence.

Siegel and Fischer (1981a, p. 7) contend that "the content of psychiatric records may reflect only the organizational policy of the agency maintaining them and not the 'true' state of affairs." Organizations may thus vary in their record keeping guidelines. In addition, service delivery facilities are subject to other requirements emanating from several sources. As a legal and financial document, certain data are required, although some institutions sometimes discourage other data from being entered. In the institutional setting, the chart is the document that is inspected for accreditation purposes and program evaluations and is also the one through which quality assurance will be assessed (Siegel & Fischer), with inadequacies brought to the attention of the clinician. With all these different interests directed at the record keeper, problems of selective reporting become quite complex.

Some institutions mandate specific guidelines for charting that must be followed by a service delivery agency to qualify for whatever benefits that institution controls. For example, The Joint Commission on the Accreditation of Healthcare Organizations has extensive requirements for facilities having or seeking accreditation. Likewise, the Office of Professional Standards Review has its own guidelines. Medicare, Medicaid, and private third-party insurers all have their requirements, which may or may not coincide with others. There may be separate guidelines for child and adolescent versus adult services; inpatient versus outpatient; agencies (usually private) heavily dependent upon third-party payment versus those (usually public) not so dependent. The more total or complete the care, the more specific the requirements tend to be (Siegel and Fischer). This may make comparisons between types of agencies problematic.

Gaynes (1989, p. 84) provides an illustration when he reports that "[clinicians] must include a diagnostic code in requests for payment." This may prompt a clinician to give a diagnosis prematurely in order for a claim to be filed. In a hospital taking third-party payments, especially those using Diagnostic Related Groups (DRGs), diagnosis is made as early and as specifically as possible. Although payment may be made on the basis of discharge diagnosis, initial diagnosis comes under scrutiny for quality control purposes. In contrast, in a public hospital not dependent upon third-party payment, early diagnosis may be very general or may be in the form of routine alternative diagnoses to be considered. Thus diagnoses made at the same time in the course of treatment may need to be interpreted very differently across sites.

Moreover, since charts are also used to justify third-party payments, the charts may contain detailed accounts of treatments, tests, and observations to conform with the specifications of the insurers. Where there is co-morbidity (more than one illness present), the primary diagnoses may be made in view of what is maximally reimbursable. For example, with Medicare and Medicaid no longer reimbursing nursing homes for the care of mentally ill patients, except those with dementia (*Hospital and Community Psychiatry*, 1988), there may be changes in primary diagnoses of the elderly so that benefits will still be available. Similar "gaming," or moral hazard effects (Feldstein, 1983), may occur in the treatment of substance abuse. Prior to 1985, DRG allowance was constructed on the basis of detoxification only, leaving the more extensive treatment programs under-reimbursed (Mezochow, Miller, Seixas, & Frances, 1987). Anecdotal evidence suggests that depression is sometimes diagnosed (which is often secondary to substance abuse) because that diagnosis has more generous reimbursements, even if the patient initially presented for the substance abuse problem.

Data other than diagnosis may also be subject to external pressures for selective reporting. Medicare specifies that progress notes for inpatients must be completed for specified time periods (Siegel & Fischer, 1981a). A psychiatrist reported to me that in her hospital setting, nurses are instructed to record bizarre behavior in patients' charts at least every 2 days or the insurance coverage stops. Obviously, this will affect the comparison of aberrant behavior across hospitals with different policies.

The extent of selective reporting due to the pressures of third-party payment is difficult to estimate. Third-party payments to psychiatry are among the lowest across medical specialties (Geis, Jesilow, Pontell, & O'Brien, 1985). However, it can also be noted that cases of fraud and abuse of federal programs are disproportionally found within psychiatry (Geis et al.). Thus, although there are fewer third-party payments made to psychiatry, there may be more gaming.

Charts are also justification for clinician decisions that may have legal implications. If violence toward self or others is at issue, some clinicians are very conservative in what they write. Furthermore, in view of malpractice, clinicians take a variety of stances on the documentation of iatrogenic illness (i.e., medical conditions caused by a treatment), such as tardive dyskinesia. Some believe that full documentation is protective; others prefer to make general entries about side effects. Such beliefs may also account for some selective reporting.

Reactivity

Archival records, such as medical charts, are said to have the advantage of being unobtrusive (Webb, Campbell, Schwartz, & Sechrest, 1966). However, under certain circumstances, these data may be quite reactive and subject to many of the same types of error inherent in survey methodologies. If they believe it to be in their best interests, patients may distort information given to the caregiver. It is also possible that some caregivers may distort (or omit) information, as suggested previously. Reactivity may be centered upon the record keeper and/or the coders, rather than the patient. If the data collection is concurrent with the record keeping, the record keeper may be affected by the knowledge that the charts are being subjected to nonroutine inspection.

Moreover, since interpretations and coding decisions made by coders are involved, a coder-based reactivity may occur. Smith et al., (1969), following the lead of Garfinkel (1967), have applied the term *ad hocing* to this problem. Where detailed coding instructions are lacking, coders will provide their own interpretations and coding rules to what they abstract from the charts. Without communication, these coding rules may be unique to individual coders, unshared among coders, or unshared between coders and researcher. The meaning of the variables may drift, eventually becoming uninterpretable.

Limitation in Variables

One obvious problem with clinical chart data is that the researcher's variables are limited by the contents of the charts. Charts typically contain some socio-demographic data, but often not in detail. Family information is usually scanty. Likewise, occupational history is usually quite sparse, preventing the measurement social mobility. Attitudinal measures are rarely found in charts. Even standardized clinical scales are not universally used.

When conceptualizing variables, one must distinguish between raw data and interpreted data in the charts. Raw data would include test scores, laboratory values, objective descriptions of behavior, as well as socio-demographic information. Interpreted data include the clinician's assessments and conclusions based upon a variety of input, not always documented. The latter type of data may be of limited use as research variables. For example, if one intends to code patient progress from progress notes, one is apt to encounter entries such as "doing fine" or "stable." Such assessments are too vague and ambiguous to have utility.

Even the diagnosis entered into a chart must be handled with caution. The researcher usually does not know, and certainly does not control, the method by which the chart diagnosis was reached. It may have been generated from a standardized instrument, such as the Diagnostic Interview Schedule; it may have been based upon the patient's history; it may have resulted from an unstructured clinical interview. It may have strictly followed DSM criteria; or it may use DSM terminology without adhering to its definitions. Thus, chart diagnosis should be conceptualized as an interpreted datum. It is the diagnostic label attached to a particular patient. As the clinician's definition of the patient's situation, it may influence how the patient will be treated, both medically and socially. However, it may not necessarily represent a specific constellation of symptoms.

Ethical Issues

There also are ethical considerations in archival data research. As mentioned previously, usually Institutional Review Boards do not require informed consent from each patient whose record is to be accessed. Care must be taken to protect confidentiality, especially when identifiers are used. Although social scientists often prefer to maintain respondent anonymity, identifying a patient by case number and name is often necessary. However, sometimes the researcher will desire an identifier that the agency may be reluctant to divulge (Hays, 1975). This issue will need to be negotiated with the agency when access is initially requested. A well-planned strategy for assuring confidentiality may help such negotiations.

Guidelines for Using Chart Data

Despite the many problems discussed above, researchers do make heavy use of clinical charts, often producing high quality data. The following are some suggestions which may improve data quality.

Consider using clinical charts in combination with other data sources (Perrucci & Targ, 1982). This may compensate for limited variables in the chart and may be a check on the accuracy of data given during patient interviews.

Learn the norms of the system and/or facility under study (Smith et al., 1969). Be a considerate guest and try to fit in with the routine. Learn the facility's filing procedures and learn which charts are not filed with the others. Also avoid the busy times at the facility; a lot of charts will be gone during that time, and the staff will appreciate your courtesy.

Some facilities have manuals that include the abbreviations and terms used in the charts. These can be quite helpful; however, do not depend upon the staff's following the manual or even knowing it. Facilities in large systems sometimes develop their own local procedures, so learn the informal conventions.

Get to know the charts before deciding whether to use them. Do not take the staff's word for what is there. You may find that certain items are never recorded, or are so consistently inaccurate that it is a waste of resources to code them.

If identifiers are necessary, record more than one if possible. Case numbers are often incorrect on the charts; individuals may have multiple case numbers, often traceable to transposed digits or poor handwriting.

Recording names helps, but also has problems. Names are altered, sometimes through marriage, but sometimes for delusional reasons. Having both numbers and names provides the opportunity for cross-checking.

Develop careful coding frames with precise definitions and priorities of information source in the event of contradictory information (Esrov,

1981). For example, what is the principal or primary diagnosis? The one given upon admission or at discharge? The one written first on a list? What happens when the order changes from one source to another? How is a diagnosis coded when it does not use standard diagnostic terminology?

Keep the coding form as simple and as concrete as possible. Require minimal coder interpretation of data to reduce "ad hocing." If possible, arrange the coding form to match the order in which the information is expected to appear in the chart. If coding from standardized forms, duplicate the order and format of the standard form for your coding form. If coding open-ended notes, have coders record exact wordings, rather than collapsing comments into a priori categories that require coder interpretation. Collapsing and categorizing can be done later, using panels of professional judges (Smith et al., 1969).

Give attention to the physical facility for the coders. Try to reserve a private workroom with easy access to the files. Never take any charts from the premises. Take time to inform the clinical and clerical staff as to the presence and the purpose of the coders.

Select coders with care. Avoid using clinic staff as coders. Although they will know the myriad recording conventions, staff members have a vested interest in the selective interpretation of entries, destroying whatever nonreactivity benefit there may be. Esrov does suggest that, wherever possible, the coders hired should have prior training in fields related to the task at hand (in this case, perhaps caseworkers, psychiatric nurses, or students training in social work, psychology, or medicine) and should also have the personality traits desired for the task: compulsive attention to detail, and the self-discipline to perform repetitive tasks consistently and accurately.

Unfortunately, the more highly qualified data collectors found chart coding unpopular and uninteresting, leading to morale problems and poor cooperation (Esrov, 1981). It is ironic that coding requiring complex steps and careful decisions can only be done well by qualified and trained personnel, who are precisely the people who become quickly bored by such repetitive work.

Train coders with the same care one would use for training interviewers. This should include training them how to behave when in contact with staff or patients. Institute periodic inter-coder reliability checks. Supervision of coders improves accuracy. The frequent presence of the principal investigator, especially if he or she actually participates in some of the coding, can raise coder accuracy and morale. This practice also keeps the researcher informed about those subtle data problems that only hands-on experience can reveal.

Smith et al. (1969) suggest using clinicians and staff to help interpret results, although the researcher need not be bound to those interpretations. Staff can provide both clinical expertise and inside knowledge of the system to enhance the meaning of findings. In addition, the inclusion of staff at this stage in the research, as well as in earlier stages, improves cooperation the next time one wishes access to that site.

In conclusion, where charts are concerned, data availability drives the conceptualization of the research question. Clearly, this is not ideal. Nevertheless, with proper precautions, clinical chart data can be useful, and even desirable, because of the low cost and relatively easy accessibility, and because charts do contain data not available elsewhere in one place, even directly from the patient.

INSTITUTIONAL STATISTICS

Computerized Medical Charts

Rather than obtaining access to individual medical charts, the researcher may be given access to computerized data bases in treatment institutions. Although a decade ago less than one-quarter of sampled treatment facilities had computerized record keeping or information systems (Siegel & Fischer, 1981c), the proportion is higher today due to the advancements in computer technology and also because of federal mandates for integrated record keeping in federally funded community mental health centers.

These data bases will have uneven quality across facilities and may not be constructed to retrieve data in a form usable in statistical analysis. Sometimes these data bases are internal to the institution, and sometimes maintenance of the data is contracted out to computer services. Whichever is the case, the researcher obviously must become very familiar with the data base before deciding whether it is serviceable. This includes knowledge about the original source of the information, the entry and updating procedures, the data base structure, and the retrieval procedures.

The contents of the computerized chart are highly selective. Areas of the medical chart receiving the most attention in these automated systems have been intake and admission, location and service status, assessment, treatment goals and strategies, services and treatments, incidents, and termination and outcomes (Laska, 1981). Some treatment facilities generate highly specialized data bases, such as hospital pharmaceutical files (Salek, 1988) and triage records (Chang, 1987). Even these could have research applications, especially if they can be linked with other data files.

The computerized data give researchers access to chart data ready for analysis without the expense and time needed for painstaking coding and data entry. However, computerized medical records have all the problems inherent in the original medical record, as discussed previously. Additionally, there is an extra intermediary. The staff who code and enter the data onto the computer are not under researcher supervision and may introduce more error into a computerized data set than would carefully trained and supervised research personnel. Hendrickson and Myers (1973) suggest that there are high rates of formal errors (i.e., logical errors that can often be detected without knowledge of the individual patient) in the computerized data bases they examined. Some of these problems are alleviated by the use of data gathering instruments especially designed for computerized systems (Spitzer & Endicott, 1971), and by data entry programs that include checks for logical errors. It is advisable to learn if your source uses such devices.

Aggregated Data

The researcher also may be able to obtain institutional data already aggregated by a treatment facility. These might include admissions rates, discharge rates, and staffing patterns. Although such data may be interesting for interorganizational comparisons, caution must be exercised here as well. Mechanic (1969), Perrucci and Targ (1982), and many others warn that aggregated statistics of this sort are produced by administrators who have agendas reflecting specific organizational needs and goals. Numbers are often produced for budgetary purposes or to justify program development, continuation, or elimination, and may reflect organizational policy more than organizational behavior (Siegel & Fischer, 1981a). In short, they may be highly politicized artifacts.

As in the case of the medical chart, one must be cognizant of the impact that economic factors, especially third-party payment, have upon the interpretation of institutional data sets. Different payment plans, such as Health Maintenance Organizations (HMOs) (Lehman, 1987) may have varying effects upon utilization and length of stay, types of patients served, and treatments (Frank & Lave, 1985; Ruby, 1984).

Just as reimbursement gamesmanship impacts the content of the clinical chart, gaming may impact institutional statistics, such as length of stay, admissions by diagnosis, and treatment modalities. Payment systems based upon diagnosis-related groups or DRGs (Goldman & Lezak, 1985) may be particularly subject to gaming strategies to maximize reimbursements or financial advantage (Fogel & Slaby, 1985). Gaming strategies may include manipulating the case mix by admitting those patients whose treatment is most cost-effective and by altering therapeutic goals to ones that are fiscally sound (Fogel & Slaby). Another gaming strategy used under Medicare is the transfer of patients from Medicare settings after benefits are exhausted to Medicare-exempt settings, either within the same facility or at a different facility entirely (Freiman & Sederer, 1990).

Because of the impact of third-party payment on so many aspects of the data, researchers comparing across treatment units often categorize these facilities into economically relevant groups. The most basic dimensions for inpatient facilities include are public versus private; psychiatric hospital versus general hospital versus substance abuse hospitals; and units that are exempt versus those not exempt from the Diagnostic Related Groups (DRG) system of reimbursement. General hospitals may also be subdivided according to the loci of psychiatric patients: on special psychiatric units versus on substance abuse units versus in scattered beds, whereby psychiatric patients are found dispersed among the nonpsychiatric patients (Freiman, Goldman, & Taube, 1990).

Not only does gaming operate to distort interpretations, but the nature of the illness or its recognition and treatment may also lead the unwary into unwarranted conclusions. For example, Stromgren (1986) warns that statistics on hospital first admissions cannot be used as estimates of the incidence of schizophrenia, as had been done in the past. Many schizophrenics do not receive that diagnosis during their first admission (given the 6-month criterion) or are never even hospitalized (given the deinstitutionalization trend). To ignore such considerations will gravely misrepresent the epidemiology of the illness. This only emphasizes the necessity of interpreting all mental illness data in light of what is known about social and economic pressures upon treatment facilities; in light of the characteristics of specific disorders; and in light of sampling biases known to occur in hospital samples (see Chapter 4).

DATA BANKS

Other sources of secondary data are the large data banks, many originating on a system level, which may be particularly useful for organizational level analysis. Leaf (1986) lists 31 such sources sponsored by the federal government, with many sponsored by divisions of the Alcohol, Drug Abuse and Mental Health Administration. Large data bases are sometimes available from insurers (Freiman & Sederer, 1990; A. Schwartz, Perlman, Paris, Schmidt, & Thornton, 1980); from states (Evenson, Cho, & Holland, 1988; Rupp, Steinwachs, & Salkever, 1985); and from other nations (Hansagi, Norell, & Magnusson, 1985; Roos & Nicol, 1981). With primary data collection costs continuing to rise, such data bases as the Veterans Administration Patient Treatment File and the National Hospital Discharge Survey, as well as Medicare/Medicaid data, will come into increased research use.

The origin of these data varies. Some data banks, such as the NIMH-sponsored Inventory of Mental Health Organizations, contain data supplied by treatment facilities. Organization data sets may be composed either of entire populations or of a sample, with participation voluntary but high (Leaf, 1986). Nevertheless, even on this level, a principal source of information is the patient discharge summary, with all the problems associated with it (Murnaghan & White, 1971). Alternatively, data sets, such as the NIMH Epidemiological Catchment Area Study or the NCH's Health and Nutrition Examination Surveys, are composed of personal interviews. Some data banks, although not restricted to mentally ill patients, are often large enough that subsamples of those treated for mental illness will contain sufficient cases for elaborate analysis.

Large data banks may be amenable to a variety of quasi-experimental designs, but without the expense and time needed for primary data collection. In particular, Roos and Nicol (1981) identify three characteristics that facilitate such use. The large number of cases permits both the retrieval of cases sharing special characteristics, and the use of multiple controls applied simultaneously. There is the potential for combining files to facilitate the development of elaborate research designs. Some data banks extend over a sufficient number of years to provide enough data points for time series analysis, with or without an intervention point.

Even with these large data banks, issues of data quality are raised. Roos, Roos, Cageorge, and Nicol (1982) suggest several ways of assessing the reliability of large data bases. These include comparing information independently recorded at different times in separate data files; searching for logical inconsistencies; and using primary data collection to check the computerized data base. As with individual medical charts, unambiguous socio-demographic and descriptive information are likely to be the most reliable data (Institute of Medicine, 1980). Using some of the methods later suggested by Roos et al., A. Schwartz et al. (1980) studied the reliability of psychiatric diagnoses in Medicaid records. They found that the diagnosis written on charts often differs from the diagnosis submitted for Medicaid claims (A. Schwartz et al.). Depending upon type of treatment facility, between 29% and 46% of the diagnoses did not match across data sources, with psychiatric outpatient clinics in general hospitals producing the most unreliable data. Likewise, depending upon treatment facility, there was most agreement between data sources for diagnoses of major psychoses, and least for substance abuse.

Hospital data bases commonly use as the unit of observation the discharge or admission, rather than the unique individual. With serious mental illness, where repeated hospitalizations are an expected part of the illness, an individual could be represented several times within one data base, even if those data cover only one year. Since this violates independence of observation assumptions, the researcher needs to be cautious in the analysis and interpretation of such information. Sometimes data bases include unique identifiers, such as patient numbers or Social Security numbers that can be used to link records, producing a data base composed of unique individuals as the unit of observation. Without such links, the denominator for hospital rates must be the episode, not the individual (Murnaghan & White, 1971).

Linking has other applications as well. Being able to link across data sets and across time can be a substantial asset. However, without common identifiers, linking can become very complex (J. Schwartz, Pieper, & Karasek, 1988). Nevertheless, the time spent in development of data files prior to analysis is usually rewarded. Kiesler, Simpkins, and Morton (1990), in their study using the Hospital Discharge Survey, demonstrate how the further development, including case weighting, of a well-recognized computerized data base needed the same care as the development of primary data. Their care resulted in stronger results than comparable studies using data not so carefully developed.

Obviously, the utility of these large data banks, as with any secondary source, rests upon their validity and reliability, as well as upon their breadth, their longitudinal characteristics, the inclusion of theoretically important variables, the detail of the methodological appendices, and the "extent to which histories of individual units can be reconstructed" (Roos & Nicol, 1981, p. 519).

CONCLUSION

Despite all the precautions necessary in the use of chart data, institutional statistics, and large data banks, these alternative data sources have an important place in research about the mentally ill population. All types of data collection carry caveats, and the ones discussed in this chapter should not be interpreted as disqualifications. After all, the deficiencies in the United States Census are well known and documented, but social scientists nevertheless find it the best source of data for some types of work. Similarly, the problems of using criminal justice statistics have been well known for a long time, yet criminologists make excellent use of them. Hospital and other institutional data can be also be utilized appropriately, if done knowledgeably.

7

Research in a Multidisciplinary Milieu

Treatment of the mentally ill is usually a multidisciplinary effort of the core mental health disciplines: psychiatry, psychology, social work, and psychiatric nursing. If a social scientist researches a mentally ill population, contact will probably be made with one or more of these disciplines. Persons in these other disciplines may function as gatekeepers, collaborators, facilitators, or even data collectors.

Much has been written about interdisciplinary conflicts and struggles over rights and responsibilities in the clinical setting. Likewise, a literature is developing on problems within the research setting. Gibson (1983), and Grady and Wallston (1988) have specifically discussed these conflicts in the health care setting. This chapter will suggest some issues and potential problems as well as the mutual benefits in multidisciplinary work in the mental health care setting. The emphasis will be upon working with the psychiatrist, because the power usually resides with the physician. However, many of the issues revolve around not only M.D./non-M.D. problems but also clinician/nonclinician differences.

WORKING WITH MULTIDISCIPLINARY TEAMS

The Medical Hierarchy

Individuals who care for the seriously mentally ill are accustomed to working in interdisciplinary, hierarchical clinical settings. Since the medical doctor is legally assigned primary medical responsibility (American Journal of Psychiatry, 1980), this invariably positions the psychiatrist at the head of the treatment team. Other mental health disciplines have charged that sometimes the team head seems to consider team members as subordinates rather than fellow professionals (Hudson, 1982).

The a priori assumption that the physician-psychiatrist is at the top of the hierarchy is sometimes carried over, albeit inappropriately, to the research setting. Conversely, social scientists in academic settings are usually accustomed to a flatter authority structure. In an academic setting, the designation of principal investigator in a research study is more often based upon who originated and developed that project, rather than replicating a power structure external to the project. Obviously, the two traditions will conflict on occasion.

It makes a big difference in the operation of the team, and particularly to the social science researcher, whether team members are employed by the facility in which the research will occur, or whether some team members come from outside the setting. Much has been written on this matter, with regard not only to health care settings (Grady & Wallston, 1988), but also more generally to wherever applied or evaluation research is done (C. Weiss, 1972). Researchers from the inside usually have easier access to data sources (Gibson, 1983; Grady & Wallston) and often have insider knowledge and understandings. However, they may also be vulnerable to pressures from those on higher bureaucratic levels and to various other role conflicts (Grady & Wallston).

Regardless of either the origins of the researchers or how the project hierarchy is arranged, the social scientist in a multidisciplinary team with mental health professionals is often a marginal person, with role relationships poorly defined at the outset. Staff in medical settings often do not understand what the behavioral scientist does, what the area of expertise is, and how that fits into the overall structure. The social scientist must continually enforce professional role definitions and clarify areas of expertise and responsibility.

Like the social sciences, all of the core mental health disciplines assign themselves research as a function. However, this does not necessarily imply formal preparation for that role. For example, the American Psychiatric Association (American Journal of Psychiatry, 1980) places promotion of research as its second objective. However, although there has been improvement in the teaching of biostatistics in medical schools (Dawson-Saunders, Azen, Greenberg, & Reed, 1987), few psychiatric training programs are known for their thoroughness of research curricula. Both self-selection and selective recruitment tend to bias psychiatry residents against seeking research training and subsequent research careers (Rancurello, 1988). Conversely, most training programs in both social work and nursing now include research components. Of course, the clinical psychologist must complete a research dissertation as part of the doctorate requirements.

Despite very obvious differences in preparation, one study (House, Miller, & Schlachter, 1978) found that there was no significant difference in how psychiatrists, psychologists, and social workers in one (nonacademic) treatment setting rated their ability to do research. However, even if persons perceive themselves capable, and even if persons have had some research experience, it should not be assumed that all members of a multidisciplinary research team share a common research knowledge base, nor that they share the same priorities vis-á-vis research, nor that they even share a similar *weltanschauung*.

Differences in Worldview

Most social scientists have had contact with related disciplines, at least during graduate training in the context of cross-listed courses—social psychology, political anthropology, political sociology. As broadening as these contacts may be, they are still within the confines of academia. The classroom is shared by students who also share a basic orientation to the scientific method and the acquisition of knowledge. Paradigms may vary, but basic commitments do not. When researching the mentally ill, one may collaborate with others who do not share those basic academic values and understandings (Dworkin, 1989a).

One basic understanding that may not be shared concerns the nature of science. Kingsbury (1987) contends that a major cognitive difference between the clinical psychologist and the psychiatrist is that the clinical psychologist, having been trained in the behavioral sciences, sees science as a method of inquiry guided by theory. The medically trained psychiatrist sees science as a system of facts, with an emphasis on the findings rather than the route by which the findings were obtained. Less concerned with theory, they tend to use science for the immediate data needed to treat the patient. These differences exist between the psychiatrist and the clinical psychologist, but they are more dramatic between the psychiatrist and the nonclinician researcher.

Psychologists are more tentative about information, and psychiatrists may seem more certain then they should be (Kingsbury, 1987). The physician may have a professional assurance that others sometimes call arrogance. Clinicians are taught to be decisive, to be confident in their abilities, and to be assured that their therapeutic technologies, however imperfect, are still better than nothing. Conversely, the social scientist lives in a world of probabilities, of skepticism and professional uncertainty. Theories are never proven; they are temporarily tenable. Methodological flaws are admitted. Put the assured medical doctor together with a probabilistic social scientist, and the latter can appear weak and insecure. Researchers must learn to have more confidence in their own special expertise and its applications, in order to present themselves as competent experts in their field, the .05 level of probability notwithstanding.

The researcher in collaboration with the clinician may also find that there are differences in the priority placed on the research protocol. Following research protocols is difficult for some clinicians, who may want to make idiosyncratic adjustments to a protocol on the basis of a patient's particular treatment needs. However, sometimes this concern for patients covers a basic aversion to the research and becomes a justification for noncooperation.

There may also be differences in the value placed upon academic freedom. Gibson (1983) suggests that some research settings may be more compatible with such values than others. He specifies that among hospitals, teaching institutions value academic freedom to a far higher degree than do individual hospitals or hospital chains. Nevertheless, in specific situations three forces may compromise the researcher's freedom: the pressures imposed by the biotechnology and pharmaceutical industries upon the collaborating academic institution (Hart, 1989); the increased concerns of the Institute of Medicine and the National Institutes of Health regarding research misconduct (Friedman, 1989); and the hierarchical nature of academic medicine. The researcher would be wise to learn at the outset if there are restrictions placed by the host institution upon the research process. This could include not only limitations in research topics, but also mandates for internal approval of proposal and/or manuscript prior to external review. Related is the question of proprietary rights to the data. To whom do the data belong? What happens to the data at the end of the study or if members of the team depart? Understandings must be reached on these matters early in a project, so that if agreement cannot be reached, the researcher may withdraw before heavy commitments have been made.

Differences in Vocabulary

The different worldview is also underscored by a different knowledge base. Just as the social scientist will have a limited understanding of the clinical experience, clinicians usually have limited knowledge of the theory and methods of social science. There is little overlap between the two literatures. The information that the clinician has about social science is likely to be dated. There may be familiarity with the work of Hollingshead and Redlich (1958), Goffman (1961), and Durkheim (1951). However, when using social science concepts such as the self-fulfilling prophecy, the clinician will often cite sources that are different from those cited by the social scientist. Likewise, in using social variables they may operationalize them in ways no longer used by social scientists. A good example of this is the clinician's measuring social class using the Hollingshead and Redlich approach, and assuming that this is the currently accepted method.

There can be troublesome misunderstandings when a common vocabulary masks very different concepts or approaches. For example, the word *interview* connotes a different process to the clinician than it does to the researcher. The clinical interview tends to be very individualized and not standardized (Collins, Given, Given, & King, 1988), in contrast to the research interview, which usually follows an interview schedule or protocol, even if the questions are open-ended. Moreover, in the clinical interview, a diagnostic impression (i.e., a hypothesis) is formed early in the interview, and then the rest of the interview is spent gathering confirmatory data only (Kraemer et al., 1987; Nurius & Gibson, 1990). Little effort is made to gather nonconfirming evidence. Even with subsequent contradictory evidence, the initial view, sometimes acquired from indirect sources, is adhered to tenaciously (Nurius & Gibson).

Similarly, the word *social* is used by clinicians often to refer to phenomena on the social psychological level. Thus, social variables will usually refer to peer pressure or stress, not organizational or societal level variables. Other words that may carry very different meanings are *basic research, paradigm, phenomenology*, and *theory*.

Educational Models

Because social science researchers on the multidisciplinary team sometimes have a tutorial role thrust upon them, it is helpful to understand the training model for the M.D. degree. The medical model of education consists of 2 full years in preclinical didactic training and then several more years of supervised clinical apprenticeship, in the form of the clerkship, internship, and residency. It is very likely that some team members may have learned about research solely as apprentices after completion of formal didactic training. The mentor role is generally defined as being more central to the research training of the psychiatrist than are formal didactic courses (Burke, Pincus, & Pardes, 1986; Rieder, 1988). Indeed, "most inexperienced researchers are usually 'turned off' by high powered, abstract presentations [of statistics]" (Gillin, 1988, p. 292). Systematic research training in psychiatry is concentrated in the research fellowships. These fellowships are limited and tend to be concentrated in only a few psychiatric research centers around the country. Less than one-third of the physicians intending a career in psychiatric research planned to take a research fellowship (Haviland, Pincus, & Dial, 1987).

Under these circumstances, training in methods and statistics for many psychiatrists attempting research can be quite haphazard, leaving knowledge gaps. To fill a gap, the physician often expects the researcher to provide a succinct answer without a prologue of background information. This may tax the capabilities of even a master teacher. Sometimes a teaching exchange, whereby each teaches the other something of his or her discipline, allows recognition of special expertise in a mutually beneficial and respectful arrangement.

Using Clinicians as Data Collectors

As discussed in chapters 3 and 6, many unstructured and semistructured diagnostic interview protocols are designed to be administered by clinicians. Furthermore, Esrov (1981) recommends using clinicians, such as nurses and social workers, to abstract data from medical charts. In this case, staff training sessions should be planned around the basic research necessities, such as following protocols precisely, as well as the particulars required in the specific research tasks to be done.

However, it is wise to avoid expecting clinicians (who are not collaborators) to do research tasks as an extra part of their job without some type of additional compensation. This includes avoiding the use of clinicians as data collectors just because they are available on site. Data collection involves paperwork. Siegel and Fischer (1981b) found that clinicians complain about the time spent on records and other routine paperwork, although the actual time spent doing such work is overestimated. If they are asked to do still more in the form of data collecting, there will be much complaining to their administrators (which is politically bad for the researcher), and much sabotage (which is methodologically bad for the research).

Coping Strategies

It is easier to identify the diverse problems associated with multidisciplinary teams than it is to suggest strategies for coping with them. To succeed in this type of setting, the traditional academic researcher will need to adapt in some fashion and to some degree. How this is done is dependent upon many variables, including one's structural position in the hierarchy; one's discipline; one's age and gender. There will also be personality factors involved. The successful strategy for one person may be incompatible with the style of another in the same situation.

There are, however, three suggestions that can be made. First, even if the project is a short-term one, treat the multidisciplinary relationship as though it were expected to be ongoing. Do not give the impression of exploiting others for a fast, single-shot data collection. Take care to develop mutual respect and courtesies. Besides making the immediate experience more pleasant for everyone, it will create the conditions for renewal of the relationships in the future, should the need arise.

Second, one should be reflective and flexible. Researchers often become so involved in the tasks of the study that they are blind to interpersonal relations. Notice what is occurring among the team and with other people touched by the research. If something is not going right, entertain the idea that interpersonal readjustments may have to be made.

Third, researchers in mental health settings, either as insiders or outsiders, need to maintain ties with other researchers of their discipline. These may be found in nearby universities, in professional associations, or in one's own department or organization. Being able to withdraw from the multidisciplinary setting into more familiar surroundings is analogous to the ethnographer's need to withdraw from the field periodically (Estroff, 1981; Goetz & LeCompte, 1984). It helps to maintain perspective and objectivity. It is a source of technical assistance and of social support as well.

GAINING ACCESS

Research involving persons with mental illness is often done in an institutional context. Mental health systems in the United States are very complex (Scott & Black, 1986) and vary by geographic region (Rosenheck & Astrachan, 1990). It is not within the scope of this book to describe the diversity of these systems; however, a researcher should learn about the system to which access is desired before approaching the designated organizational official who can award access. This gatekeeper is an important personage, regardless of whether the researcher is an insider to the system or an outsider. Gatekeepers' reactions to proposed research may vary according to whether they have a clinical or an administration/business background.

Even if the researcher is an insider, access cannot be automatically assumed. Good relationships with the gatekeeper must be cultivated if permissions, support, and resources are to be forthcoming. For the outsider, it will be worth the time to learn as much as possible about the organization prior to seeking access to it. In particular, it would be useful to know what kinds of intramural and extramural research (if any) it has hosted in the past. Past experience with research does not guarantee hospitality. The administration of an organization accustomed to hosting medical studies may have quite different attitudes toward biomedical research than toward social science research, which is generally seen as lower in prestige.

The gatekeeper may attempt to exercise control over research topic, design, or focus. Researchers must decide what research bargains, if any, they are willing to negotiate in return for gaining access. Some administrators may be more amenable to research if they are included in the initial planning. When researchers can create projects with theoretical importance and good design that also address administrative concerns and priorities, access may be more freely given.

The clinician/administrator is often protective toward patients and may be reluctant to sanction their participation as research subjects. Furthermore, public accountability may make an administrator hesitate to authorize any experimentation, for fear of being accused of permitting patients to be used as "guinea pigs." The researcher must be prepared to answer the question: "How will this research help me (or my organization) better treat patients?" Unfortunately, this question often masks an equally real one: "How will this research get me, the administrator, into trouble?" This question is going to be salient with any invasive experimental design. It will be even more salient with research done on the organizational level of analysis. Regardless of the motivations of the researcher, a study that has the potential of documenting organizational deficiencies may be seen as too threatening to sanction.

Prior to granting access, the administrator will want to know the costs and benefits to the patients as well as to the organization. The researcher should be prepared to give a realistic estimate of what the research will cost the organization in terms of time, money, personnel, and other resources, including office space and supplies. Likewise, the researcher should be prepared to discuss some expected benefits. These may be in the form of written reports, presentations to administrative staff and governing boards, or in-service workshops for clinical staff. If these products can be linked to improved patient care and/or increased cost-effectiveness of programs, the case for access will be all the stronger. Not only will access be more readily obtained if the research promises more benefits than costs to the organization, but if these promises are fulfilled, future access will be even easier.

Interlude

Even when access is granted by a centralized administration, there may be problems on the local level. The attitude of the facility director is an important factor in the success of research done in any treatment facility (Young, 1986). The following example illustrates how failure to gain the cooperation of local administrators, and then expecting clinicians to do data collection, resulted in a ruined design.

As part of a study, I needed a two-page structured interview administered to new patients during intake at five outpatient clinics over the course of one month. This would have involved approximately 20 intakes per clinic. The five clinics all drew from the same population of chronic patients newly discharged from inpatient treatment. Allocation to the clinics was made on the basis of geographic location. The medical directors of three of the facilities immediately agreed to cooperate, observing that they routinely asked many of the items anyway. The other two refused on the basis that they did not have the time, and that such an interview could compromise the development of the proper therapeutic alliance. The two reluctant medical directors yielded only when their supervisor mandated participation.

As a compromise, I agreed that the interview would not be done if a patient appeared too psychotic. This seemed to be a reasonable arrangement, since data from an acutely psychotic patient would not be reliable anyway. Furthermore, since these patients had just been discharged from the hospital, nearly all were expected to be relatively stable. I expected to lose very few respondents. At the end of the month of data collection, response rates were computed. The three clinics with cooperating directors had response rates between 90% and 96%. The other two clinics had response rates of 35% and 40%. With such different response rates, it is clear that the data from the two uncooperative clinics would contain serious biases. Those clinics were subsequently deleted from the study. The lesson is that when clinicians are forced to participate in research, the researcher loses. Participation does not necessarily imply cooperation.

WRITING FOR DIFFERENT AUDIENCES

Working on multidisciplinary teams will eventuate in researchers writing for several different audiences and sometimes publishing in journals outside the social scientist's home discipline. Applied work finds audiences outside the academy in the readership of clinical journals. Another audience is composed of policymakers, administrators, and boards of trustees. These audiences are not especially concerned with the testing of basic theory; they are seeking understandable, relevant, and timely data that can be used when decisions must be made or patients must be treated.

The production of reports and papers is the occasion for differences and conflicts on the multidisciplinary team. One difference is in the traditions of awarding authorship. Papers published in social science journals tend to have between one and three authors. In contrast, it is less common for a paper published in a medical journal to have as few as three authors. Those that do generally are not reporting empirical findings, but are literature reviews, case studies, or opinion pieces. Reich, Black, and Jarjoua (1987) found that the mean number of authors publishing in two major psychiatry journals has been increasing over the past 30 years and in 1983 reached 3.37, an average that includes reviews and case studies. Indeed, there are published articles that literally have more authors than pages. Some critics decry the ritual inclusion as authors of various individuals who have not directly participated in the writing of the paper (Woolf, 1987). Nevertheless, it still is a common practice to include as authors people who may have had little direct input into the manuscript. Reich et al. speculate that some of the increase in number of authors may be due to increases in technical and clinical personnel needed for studies, as well as in increased publishing pressures in medical schools. The matter of authorship in most multidisciplinary teams will be an issue that must be handled with delicacy due to varying traditions, bureaucratic expectations, and academic pressures.

Reporting styles differ greatly across disciplines. Obviously referencing styles vary, but there are also other differences that make a manuscript prepared for one journal not appropriate for another. Clinical journals typically print shorter articles. Generally, they contain very brief literature reviews and usually have no specific theory section. If theories are included, they tend to be predictive, not explanatory. The focus is upon practical application. The basic social scientist may have considerable difficulty accommodating to the applied focus (Rossi & Whyte, 1983) and may need to rely upon others on the team to advise and assist.

Another difference is in the attitude toward statistics and the ways they are used. To the researcher trained in applied statistics, the analyses contained in many medical journals will seem superficial. Much tabular space is occupied by descriptive data. In the case of small sample sizes, the raw data on every case are sometimes presented in one large table. Noteworthy is the almost exclusive use of significance tests, especially student's t-tests; analysis of variance exclusive of interaction effects; and vague chi-square tests (Salsburg, 1985). Regression techniques are often denigrated as only correlational.

Furthermore, published articles frequently contain obvious statistical errors (Davies, 1987; Salsburg, 1985). The magnitude of the probability value sometimes seems to be mistaken for effect size. Sample sizes are often very small, reducing the power of the tests (Davies). Strings of bivariate statistics tend to be used when multivariate techniques are appropriate (Davies).

Occasionally, there are attempts to turn inadequacies into virtues. Simplicity is sometimes equated with honesty and usefulness. Clinicians sometimes argue that using multivariate techniques, statistical controls, and curvilinear analyses, constitute "data massaging" and that these techniques are misleading and suspicious. However, the clinician's preference for simplicity creates problems for the scientist. Psychosocial researchers in mental illness deal with very complex phenomena, as do most social scientists. There becomes a problem of how to balance both the necessity of complex techniques to understand complex relationships, and the necessity to make the presentation comprehensible to the statistically uninitiated (Dworkin, 1989a). That is, how does one keep it simple but not simplistic?

Some clinical journals are stretching their readers with multivariate techniques. Multiple regression is gaining some favor, and MANOVA is found in the more psychologically oriented journals. In particular, logistic regression and discriminant function are coming into wider use because of their applicability in situations with dichotomous dependent variables, which are so often the interest of the clinician.

OPPORTUNITIES AND CONTRIBUTIONS

Contributions by Social Science

The social sciences have many contributions to make to the study of the mentally ill. Challenging the implicit causal order in the biopsychosocial model and designing appropriate studies to test hypotheses of causal process is one area of high priority. Broadening the concept of social and environmental factors is another theoretical area in which the social scientist may lead (Dworkin, 1991). Social and environmental factors are usually defined as interpersonal ones, reflecting the disciplinary bias of psychiatrists and psychologists. The focus on the interpersonal is exemplified by theories placing the etiology of schizophrenia on some abnormality within the family. The recent life events approach represents another limited definition of the social factors implicated in depression and other mental illness.

Dunner (1988) has pointed out that psychiatric research needs to consider environment in a broader way than merely as interpersonal life events. Psychiatry has yet to acquire this broader perspective, but the social sciences already have developed a large literature in that area. A recent example is Warner's (1985) study of how political and economic trends affect hospitalization and discharge rates of patients diagnosed with schizophrenia.

Social mobility (Fox, 1991), race and culture (Dworkin & Adams, 1987; Windle, 1980), and occupational characteristics (Link, Dohrenwend, & Skiodol, 1986) are a few of the social variables that continue to be promising avenues of theory development. These social variables need not be expected to explain all the variance, as older theories unsuccessfully attempted to do. The burden of explanation is shared in models that posit social, psychological, and biological variables interrelating in complex ways.

Social science also can lead in the study of underresearched populations. With the psychiatric focus upon clinical populations, there are other groups of people relevant to an understanding of mental illness who have not been studied. These include people with symptoms of mental illness who are outside the psychiatric context. People who seek help from alternative sources, such as family physicians, clergy, or folk healers have been identified in epidemiological studies, but have not been studied intensively. False positives and false negatives are two groups who have been neglected in research about mental illness. It has been assumed that false identifications in case finding studies are merely instances of measurement error. However, as Armstrong (1987) points out, they can be theoretically interesting. Representative of the group of false positives are some homeless people who commit themselves to psychiatric hospitals for shelter rather than for treatment (Snow, Baker, & Anderson, 1988).

Social science can make contributions to the study of mental illness in the methodological arena as well. Being facile in a wide variety of methodologies, the social scientist can design studies that better address research questions than can those who are limited to clinical trial methodology. Social scientists are skilled in developing and managing large data sets. They also are trained in understanding complex relationships through the use of multivariate statistics.

Another potential contribution lies in the selection of controls. The mental health professional concentrates on the population in treatment so that controls in experimental designs tend to be people with other diagnoses, rather than people who are not ill. The obvious pitfall lies in the problematic validity and reliability of diagnosis, sometimes forcing comparisons between arbitrarily defined groups.

With most of the psychiatric research limited to the ill, there is little understanding of how the disordered differ from the normal. Without the normal comparison, conditional variables are not explored, and treatment and prevention strategies become ill advised. However, social scientists are interested both in what makes people ill and in what keeps people well, what draws some people into treatment and what keeps some away. Thus, the use of normal controls will improve both designs and theory.

Contributions to Social Science

Leona Bachrach (1987), a sociologist responsible for introducing many sociological concepts into the psychiatric literature, contends that the two disciplines are naturally compatible and that psychiatry has much to gain from a coalition with sociology, given what the latter can contribute. Being aware of some of the many problems encountered when working within a multidisciplinary setting, one may wonder why social scientists would elect to participate in collaborative studies. Making contributions to another discipline such as psychiatry is commendable, but the relationship must be reciprocal. For sustained and egalitarian research coalitions, social science must have lasting disciplinary interest in the substantive topic.

Indeed, scholarly interest in the mentally ill is not confined to mental health professionals. Social science has its own theoretical and substantive investment in the field. Studying the mentally ill may provide insights not only into mental illness, but also into other sociological issues. The nature of deviance and societal reactions to deviance; how organizations work; and the political and economic imperatives in the development and changes in public service institutions are but a few of the social phenomena that can be better understood with a comprehension of the mentally ill. Focusing upon this population ought not be the exclusive realm of medical sociologists, and it should not be limited only to those whose training is from clinical disciplines. Just as research on norm violators and deviants has better informed social scientists about the greater population who conform to norms, and just as a study of cross-national issues provides a viable frame of reference for those who study a single society, the study of the mentally ill better informs social research about the rest of the society.

References

Abrams, R. (1988). Dementia research in the nursing home. *Hospital and Community Psychiatry, 39*, 257-259.

Adams, G. L., Dworkin, R. J., & Knox, D. K. (1985). Polypharmacy in the public sector care of ambulatory chronic patients. In R. C. Chacko (Ed.), *The chronic mental patient in a community context* (pp. 41-56). Washington, DC: American Psychiatric Press.

American Journal of Psychiatry. (1980). Guidelines for psychiatrists in consultative, supervisory, or collaborative relationships with nonmedical therapists. *American Journal of Psychiatry, 137*, 1489-1491.

American Psychiatric Association. (1980). *Diagnostic and statistical manual of mental disorders* (3rd ed.). Washington, DC: Author.

American Psychiatric Association. (1987). *Diagnostic and statistical manual of mental disorders* (3rd ed., rev.). Washington, DC: Author.

American Psychiatric Association Commission on Psychotherapies. (1982). *Psychotherapy Research: Methodological and efficacy issues*. Washington, DC: American Psychiatric Association.

Anderson, J. C., Williams, S., McGee, R., & Silva, P. A. (1987). Disorders in preadolescent children. *Archives of General Psychiatry, 44*, 69-76.

Andreasen, N. C. (1988). Brain imaging: Application in psychiatry. *Science, 239*, 1381-1388.

Andreasen, N. C., Endicott, J., Spitzer, R. L., & Winokur, G. (1977). The family history method using diagnostic criteria: Reliability and validity. *Archives of General Psychiatry, 34*, 1229-1235.

Andreasen, N. C., Rice, J., Endicott, J., Reich, T., & Coryell, W. (1986). The family history approach to diagnosis. *Archives of General Psychiatry, 43*, 421-429.

Aneshensel, C. (1985). The natural history of depressive symptoms: Implications for psychiatric epidemiology. In J. R. Greenley (Ed.), *Research in community and mental health: A research annual* (Vol. 5). Greenwich, CT: JAI Press.

Annas, G. J., & Glantz, L. H. (1986). Rules for research in nursing homes [Letter to the editor]. *New England Journal of Medicine, 315*, 1157-1158.

Annas, G. J., Glantz, L. H., & Katz, B. F. (1977). *Informed consent to human experimentation: The subjects' dilemma*. Cambridge MA: Ballinger.

Anthony, J. C., Folstein, M., Romanoski, A. J., Von Korff, M. R., Nestadt, G. R., Chahal, R., Merchant, A., Brown, C. H., Shapiro, S., Kramer, M., & Gruenberg, E. M. (1985). Comparison of the lay Diagnostic Interview Schedule and a standardized psychiatric diagnosis: Experience in eastern Baltimore. *Archives of General Psychiatry, 42*, 667-675.

Antonovsky, A. (1979). *Health, stress, and coping*. San Francisco: Jossey-Bass.

Arluke, A. (1988). The sick role concept. In D. S. Gochman (Ed.), *Health behavior: Emerging research perspectives* (pp. 169-180). New York: Plenum.

Armstrong, D. (1987). Theoretical tensions in biopsychosocial medicine. *Social Science and Medicine, 25,* 1213-1218.

Ashely, B. M. (1975). Ethics of experimenting with persons. In J. C. Schoolar & C. M. Gaitz (Eds.), Research and the psychiatric patient (pp. 15-30). New York: Brunner/Mazel.

Babbie, E. (1989). The practice of social research (5th ed.). Belmont, CA: Wadsworth.

Bachrach, L. L. (1976). *Deinstitutionalization: An analytical review and sociological perspective* (DHEW Publication No. ADM 76-351). Washington DC: Government Printing Office.

Bachrach, L. L. (1987). Sociological thought in psychiatric care. *Hospital and Community Psychiatry, 38,* 819-820.

Bachrach, L. L. (1988). Defining chronic mental illness: A concept paper. *Hospital and Community Psychiatry, 39,* 383-388.

Baekeland, F., & Lundwall, L. (1975). Dropping out of treatment: A critical review. *Psychiatric Bulletin, 82,* 738-783.

Baldessarini, R. J., Katz, B., & Cotton, P. (1984). Dissimilar dosing with high-potency and low-potency neuroleptics. *American Journal of Psychiatry, 141,* 748-752.

Barber, B. (1980). *Informed consent in medical therapy and research.* New Brunswick, NJ: Rutgers University Press.

Barchas, J. D., King, R., & Berger, P. A. (1984). Neuroregulators and schizophrenia: A look at the dopamine and endorphin hypotheses. In H. C. Stancer, P. E. Garfinkel, & V. M. Rakaff (Eds.), *Guidelines for the use of psychotropic drugs* (pp. 261-276). New York: Spectrum.

Barrett, J., & Rose, R. M. (Eds.). (1986). *Mental disorders in the community: Progress and challenge.* New York: Guilford Press.

Bassuk, E. (1984). The homeless problem. *Scientific American, 251,* 40-45.

Bateson, G., Jackson, D. D., Haley, J., & Weakland, J. (1956). Toward a theory of schizophrenia. *Behavioral Science, 1,* 251-264.

Beck, A. T., Ward, C. H., Mendelson, M., Mock, J., & Erbaugh, J. (1961). An inventory for measuring depression. *Archives of General Psychiatry, 4,* 53-63.

Becker, M. H. (1974). The health belief model and sick role behavior. *Health Education Monograph, 2,* 409-419.

Becker, M. H., & Maiman, L. A. (1975). Sociobehavioral determinants of compliance with health and medical care recommendations. *Medical Care, 13,* 10-24.

Bell, R. A., Kelly, K. A., Clements, R. D., Warheit, G. J., & Holzer, C. E. (1976). Alcoholism, life events, and psychiatric impairment. *Annals of the New York Academy of Sciences, 273,* 467-480.

Benfield, C. Y., Palmer, D. J., Pfefferbaum, B., & Stowe, M. L. (1988). A comparison of depressed and nondepressed children on measures of attributional style, hopelessness, life stress, and temperament. *Journal of Abnormal Child Psychology, 16,* 397-410.

Berg, B. L. (1989). *Qualitative research methods for the social sciences.* Boston: Allyn & Bacon.

Berkman, L. F. (1984). Assessing the physical health effects of social networks and social support. *Annual Review of Public Health, 5,* 413-432.

Berkman, L. F. (1986). Social networks, support, and health: Taking the next step forward. *American Journal of Epidemiology, 123,* 559-562.

Berkson, J. (1946). Limitations of the application of fourfold table analysis to hospital data. *Biometrics Bulletin, 2,* 47-53.

Berner, P., Katschnig, H., & Lenz, G. (1986). The polydiagnostic approach in research on schizophrenia. In A. M. Freedman, R. Brotman, I. Silverman, & D. Hutson (Eds.), *Issues in psychiatric classification* (pp. 70-91). New York: Human Sciences Press.

Birchwood, M. J., Hallett, S. E., & Preston, M. C. (1989). *Schizophrenia.* New York: New York University Press.

Bowlby, J. (1988). Developmental psychiatry comes of age. *American Journal of Psychiatry, 145,* 1-10.

Bradburn, N. M., & Sudman, S. (1979). *Improving interview method and questionnaire design.* San Francisco: Jossey-Bass.

Broadhead, W. E., Kaplan, B. H., James, S. A., Wagner, E. H., Schoenback, V. J., Grimson, R., Heyden, S., Tibblin, G., & Gehlbach, S. H. (1983). The epidemiological evidence for a relationship between social support and health. *American Journal of Epidemiology, 117,* 521-537.

Bromet, E. J., Dunn, L. O., Connell, M. M., Dew, M. A., & Schulberg, H. C. (1986). Long term reliability of diagnosing lifetime major depression in a community setting. *Archives of General Psychiatry, 43,* 435-440.

Brown, P. (1985). *The transfer of care: Psychiatric deinstitutionalization and its aftermath.* London: Routledge & Kegan Paul.

Burke, J. D., Pincus, H. A., & Pardes, H. (1986). The clinician-researcher in psychiatry. *American Journal of Psychiatry, 143,* 968-975.

Cameron, O. G. (Ed.). (1987). *Presentations of depression.* New York: John Wiley.

Campbell, D. T., & Fiske, D. W. (1959). Convergent and discriminant validation by the multitrait-multimethod matrix. *Psychological Bulletin, 56,* 81-105.

Campbell, D. T., & Stanley, J. C. (1963). *Experimental and quasi-experimental designs for research.* Chicago: Rand McNally.

Canfield, M., Clarkin, J., Coyne, L., & Grob, M. (1986). Reliability of data taken from medical charts. *The Psychiatric Hospital, 17,* 173-179.

Cannell, C. F., Oksenberg, L., & Converse, J. M. (1977). *Experiments in interviewing techniques: Field experiments in health reporting 1971-1977.* Ann Arbor, MI: Survey Research Center, Institute for Social Research.

Carpenter, W. T., & Hanlon, T. E. (1986). Clinical practice and the phenomenology of schizophrenia. In G. D. Burrows, T. R. Norman, & G. Rubinstein (Eds.), *Handbook of studies in schizophrenia, part I* (pp. 123-134). Amsterdam: Elsevier Science.

Casper, E. S. (1987). A management system to maximize compliance with standards for medical records. *Hospital and Community Psychiatry, 38,* 1191-1194.

Chang, M. M. (1987). Clinician-entered computerized psychiatric triage records. *Hospital and Community Psychiatry, 38,* 652-656.

Charney, E. A., & Weissman, M. M. (1988). Epidemiology of depressive illness. In J. J. Mann (Ed.), *Phenomenology of depressive illness* (pp. 45-74). New York: Human Sciences Press.

Chesney, A. P., Larson, D., Brown, K., & Bunce, H. (1981). A comparison of patient self-report and physicians' observations in a psychiatric outpatient clinic. *Journal of Psychiatric Research, 16,* 173-182.

Christie, K. A., Burke, J. D., Jr., Regier, D. A., Raie, D. S., Boyd, J. H., & Locke, B. Z. (1988). Epidemiologic evidence for early onset of mental disorders and higher risk of drug abuse in young adults. *American Journal of Psychiatry, 145,* 971-975.

Ciompi, L. (1980). Catamnestic long-term study on the course of life and aging of schizophrenics. *Schizophrenia Bulletin, 6,* 606-618.

Clausen, G. T. (1972). Some problems of design and inference in studies of community tenure. *Journal of Nervous and Mental Disease, 155*, 22-35.

Clayton, P. J. (1986). Bipolar illness. In G. Winokur & P. Clayton (Eds.), *The medical basis of psychiatry* (pp. 39-59). Philadelphia: W. B. Saunders.

Cleary, P. D., Mechanic, D., & Weiss, N. (1981). The effect of interviewer characteristics on responses to a mental health interview. *Journal of Health and Social Behavior, 22*, 183-193.

Cockerham, W. C. (1989). *Sociology of mental disorder.* Englewood Cliffs, NJ: Prentice-Hall.

Cohen, M. R., & Winokur, G. (1988). The clinical classification of depressive disorders. In J. J. Mann (Ed.), *Phenomenology of depressive illness* (pp. 75-96). New York: Human Sciences Press.

Cohen, P. R. (1988). The effects of instruments and informants on ascertainment. In D. L. Dunner, E. S. Gershon, & J. E. Barrett (Eds.), *Relatives at risk for mental disorder* (pp. 31-52). New York: Raven Press.

Collins, C., Given, B., Given, C. W., & King, S. (1988). Interviewer training and supervision. *Nursing Research, 37*, 122-124.

Cook, T. D., & Campbell, D. T. (1979). *Quasi-experimentation: Design and analysis issues for field settings.* Chicago: Rand McNally.

Corcoran, K., & Fischer, J. (1987). *Measures for clinical practice: A sourcebook.* New York: Free Press.

Coryell, W., & Winokur, G. (1982). Course and outcome. In E. S. Payket (Ed.), *Handbook of affective disorders* (pp. 93-106). New York: Guilford Press.

Cosper, R. (1969). Interview bias in a study of drinking practices. *Quarterly Journal of Studies on Alcohol, 30*, 152-157.

Coverdale, J. H., & Aruffo, J. A. (1989). Family planning needs of female chronic psychiatric outpatients. *American Journal of Psychiatry, 146*, 1489-1491.

Crow, T. J. (1990). Structural changes in the brain in schizophrenia. In A. Kales, C. N. Stefanis, & J. A. Talbott (Eds.), *Recent advances in schizophrenia* (pp. 81-94). New York: Springer-Verlag.

Davidson, C. V., & Davidson, R. H. (1983). The significant other as data source and data problem in psychotherapy outcome research. In M. J. Lambert, E. R. Christensen, & S. S. DeJulio (Eds.), *The assessment of psychotherapy outcome* (pp. 569-602). New York: John Wiley.

Davies, J. (1987). A critical survey of scientific methods in two psychiatry journals. *Australian and New Zealand Journal of Psychiatry, 21*, 367-373.

Davis, J. M. (1974). Dose equivalence of the anti-psychotic drugs. *Journal of Psychiatric Research, 11*, 65-69.

Davis, J. M., Janicak, P. G., & Andriukaitis, S. M. (1986). Scientific and pragmatic considerations for naming and classifying psychiatric disorders. In A. M. Freedman, R. Brotman, I. Silverman, & D. Hutson (Eds.), *Issues in psychiatric classification* (pp. 92-110). New York: Human Sciences Press.

Dawson-Saunders, B., Azen, S., Greenberg, R. S., & Reed, A. H. (1987). The instruction of biostatistics in medical schools. *The American Statistician, 41*, 263-266.

Day, R. (1986). Social stress and schizophrenia: From the concept of recent life events to the notion of toxic environments. In G. D. Burrows, T. R. Norman, & G. Rubinstein (Eds.), *Handbook of studies in schizophrenia, part I* (pp. 71-82). Amsterdam: Elsevier Science.

Denzin, N. K., & Spitzer, S. P. (1966). Paths to the mental hospital and staff predictions of patient role behavior. *Journal of Health and Social Behavior, 7*, 265-271.

Devins, G. M., & Orme, C. M. (1985). Centre for epidemiological studies depression scale. In D. J. Keyser & R. C. Sweetland (Eds.), *Test critiques* (vol. 2, pp. 144-160). Kansas City, MO: Test Corporation of America.

Dilley, J. W., Ochitill, H. N., Perl, M., & Volberding, P. A. (1985). Findings in psychiatric consultations with patients with acquired immune deficiency syndrome. *American Journal of Psychiatry, 142*, 82-86.

DiMatteo, M. R., & DiNicola, D. D. (1982). *Achieving patient compliance: The psychology of the medical practitioner's role.* Elmsford, NY: Pergamon.

DiMatteo, M. R., & Friedman, H. S. (1982). *Social psychology and medicine.* Cambridge, MA: Oelgeschlager.

Dohrenwend, B. P. (1983). The epidemiology of mental disorder. In D. Mechanic (Ed.), *Handbook of health, health care, and the health professions* (pp. 157-194). New York: Free Press.

Dorland's medical dictionary, shorter edition. (1980). Philadelphia: W. B. Saunders.

Dumont, M. P. (1987). A diagnostic parable (1st ed., unrev.). *Readings: A Journal of Reviews and Commentary in Mental Health, 2*, 9-12.

Dunner, D. L. (1988). High-risk studies: The impact of research designs on research results. In D. L. Dunner, E. S. Gershon, & J. E. Barrett (Eds.), *Relatives at risk for mental disorder* (pp. 65- 71). New York: Raven Press.

Durkheim, E. (1951). *Suicide: A study in sociology.* Glencoe, IL: Free Press of Glencoe.

Dworkin, R. J. (1987). Hidden bias in the use of archival data. *Evaluation and the Health Professions, 10*, 173-185.

Dworkin, R. J. (1989a). *Vanishing borders: Sociologist on the edge.* Presentation made to Southwest Sociological Association Annual Meetings.

Dworkin, R. J. (1989b). Interviewer preferences for respondent groups. *Evaluation and the Health Professions, 12*, 282-299.

Dworkin, R. J. (1991). *On the meaning of "social" in the biopsychosocial model of mental illness.* Presented at the Southwest Sociological Association Annual Meetings.

Dworkin, R. J., & Adams, G. L. (1987). Retention of Hispanics in public sector mental health services. *Community Mental Health Journal, 23*, 204-216.

Dworkin, R. J., & Dworkin, A. G. (1989). *Interviewer attitudes about the mentally ill.* Unpublished manuscript.

Dworkin, R. J., Friedman, L. R., Telschow, R. L., Grant, K., Moffic, H. S., & Sloan, V. (1990). The longitudinal use of the global assessment scale in multiple-rater situations. *Community Mental Health Journal, 26*, 331-340.

Eaton, W. W. (1986). The epidemiology of schizophrenia. In G. D. Burrows, T. R. Norman, & G. Rubinstein (Eds.), *Handbook of studies in schizophrenia, part I* (pp. 11-33). Amsterdam: Elsevier Science.

Eisen, S. V., Grob, M. C., & Klein, A. A. (1986). BASIS: The development of a self-report measure for psychiatric inpatient evaluation. *The Psychiatric Hospital 17*, 165-171.

Endicott, J., Andreasen, N., & Spitzer, R. L. (1975). *Family history—Research diagnostic criteria.* New York: Biometrics Research, New York State Psychiatric Institute.

Endicott, J., & Spitzer, R. L. (1978). A diagnostic interview: The Schedule for Affective Disorders and Schizophrenia. *Archives of General Psychiatry, 35*, 837-844.

Endicott, J., Spitzer, R. L., Fleiss, J. L., & Cohen, J. (1976). The global assessment scale: A procedure for measuring overall severity of psychiatric disturbance. *Archives of General Psychiatry, 33*, 766-771.

Engel, G. L. (1977). The need for a new medical model: A challenge for biomedicine. *Science, 196*, 129-196.

Esrov, L. V. (1981). Assuring data quality in services evaluation. In P. M. Wortman (Ed.), *Methods for evaluating health services* (pp. 23-40). Beverly Hills, CA: Sage.

Estroff, S. E. (1981). *Making it crazy.* Berkeley: University of California Press.

Evenson, R. C., Cho, D. W., & Holland, R. (1988). Identifying psychiatric suicides for research purposes. *Journal of Clinical Psychology, 44*, 1029-1032.

Faris, R. E. L., & Dunham, H. W. (1939). *Mental disorders in urban areas.* Chicago: University of Chicago Press.

Faulstich, M. E. (1987). Psychiatric aspects of AIDS. *American Journal of Psychiatry, 144*, 551-556.

Feighner, J. P., Robins, E., Guze, S. B., Woodruff, R. A., Winokur, G., & Munoz, R. (1972). Diagnostic criteria for use in psychiatric research. *Archives of General Psychiatry, 26*, 57-63.

Feinstein, A. R. (1985). *Clinical epidemiology: The architecture of clinical research.* Philadelphia: W. B. Saunders.

Feldstein, P. J. (1983). *Health care economics* (2nd ed.). New York: John Wiley.

Felton, B. J. (1982). The aged: Settings, services, and needs. In L. R. Snowden (Ed.), *Reaching the underserved* (pp. 23-42). Beverly Hills, CA: Sage.

Fessel, W. J., & Van Brunt, E. E. (1972). Assessing quality of care from the medical record. *The New England Journal of Medicine, 286*, 134-138.

Fogel, B. S., & Slaby, A. E. (1985). Beyond gamesmanship: Strategies for coping with prospective payment. *Hospital and Community Psychiatry, 36*, 760-763.

Folstein, M. F., Folstein, S. E., & McHugh, P. R. (1975). "Mini-mental status": A practical method for grading the cognitive state of patients for the clinician. *Journal of Psychiatric Research, 12*, 189-198.

Fox, J. W. (1991). Social class, mental illness, and social mobility: The social selection-drift hypothesis for serious mental illness. *Journal of Health and Social Behavior, 31*, 344-353.

Frank, R. G., & Lave, J. R. (1985). The impact of Medicaid benefit design on length of hospital stay and patient transfers. *Hospital and Community Psychiatry, 36*, 749-753.

Frazier, S. H. (1985). NIMH reorganization focuses on specific disorders, basic science, and research training. *Hospital and Community Psychiatry, 36*, 1265-1266, 1270.

Freedman, A. M., Brotman, R., Silverman, I., & Hutson, D. (Eds.). (1986). *Issues in psychiatric classification.* New York: Human Sciences Press.

Freiman, M. P., Goldman, H. H., & Taube, C. A. (1990). Hospitalization for psychiatric illness under Medicare, 1985. *Hospital and Community Psychiatry, 41*, 51-58.

Freiman, M. P., & Sederer, L. I. (1990). Transfers of hospitalized psychiatric patients under Medicare's prospective payment system. *American Journal of Psychiatry, 147*, 100-105.

Friedman, P. J. (1989). A last call for self-regulation of biomedical research. *Academic Medicine, 64*, 502-504.

Garfield, S. L., Prager, R. A., & Bergin, A. E. (1971). Evaluation of outcome on psychotherapy. *Journal of Consulting and Clinical Psychology, 37*, 307-313.

Garfield, S. L., Prager, R. A., & Bergin, A. E. (1974). Some further comments on evaluation of outcome on psychotherapy. *Journal of Consulting and Clinical Psychology, 42*, 296-297.

Garfinkel, H. (1967). *Studies in ethnomethodology.* Englewood Cliffs, NJ: Prentice-Hall.

Gaynes, M. J. (1989). Civil monetary penalties law: Mistakes could be (very) costly. *Texas Medicine, 85*, 83-85.

Gehlbach, S. H. (1979). Comparing methods of data collection in an academic ambulatory practice. *Journal of Medical Education, 54*, 730-732.

Geis, G., Jesilow, P., Pontell, H., & O'Brien, M. J. (1985). Fraud and abuse of government medical benefit programs by psychiatrists. *American Journal of Psychiatry, 142*, 231-234.

Gershon, E. S., & Guroff, J. J. (1984). Information from relatives: Diagnosis of affective disorders. *Archives of General Psychiatry, 41*, 173-180.

Gibbon, M., McDonald-Scott, P., & Endicott, J. (1981). Mastering the art of research interviewing: A model training procedure for diagnostic evaluation. *Archives of General Psychiatry, 38*, 1259-1262.

Gibson, G. (1983). Health services research. In H. E. Freeman, R. R. Dynes, P. H. Rossi, & W. F. Whyte (Eds.), *Applied sociology*, (pp. 215-233). San Francisco: Jossey-Bass.

Gillin, J. C. (1988). Postresidency research training of psychiatrists. *Psychopharmacology Bulletin, 24*, 291-292.

Gochman, D. S. (1988). Cognitive determinants. In D. S. Gochman (Ed.), *Health behavior: Emerging research perspectives* (pp. 21-26). New York: Plenum.

Goetz, J. P., & LeCompte, M. D. (1984). *Ethnography and qualitative design in educational research.* Orlando, FL: Academic Press.

Goffman, E. (1961). *Asylums.* Garden City, NY: Doubleday.

Goldman, H. H. (1984). The chronically ill: Who are they? Where are they? In M. Mirabi (Ed.), *The chronically mentally ill: Research and services* (pp. 33-44). New York: Spectrum.

Goldman, H. H. (1988). *Review of general psychiatry* (2nd ed.). Norwalk, CT: Appleton & Lange.

Goldman, H. H., Gattozzi, A. A., & Taube, C. A. (1981). Defining and counting the chronically mentally ill. *Hospital and Community Psychiatry, 32*, 21-27.

Goldman, H. H., & Lezak, A. D. (1985). Diagnosis related groups and prospective payment in psychiatric hospital care. In S. S. Sharfstein & A. Beigel (Eds.), *The new economics and psychiatric care* (pp. 105-118). Washington DC: American Psychiatric Press.

Gottschalk, L. A. (1990). The psychotherapies in the context of new developments in the neurosciences and biological psychiatry. *American Journal of Psychotherapy, 64*, 321-339.

Gove, W. R. (1982). The current status of the labelling theory of mental illness. In W. R. Gove (Ed.), *Deviance and mental illness* (pp. 273-300). Beverly Hills, CA: Sage.

Grady, K. E., & Wallston, B. S. (1988). *Research in health care settings.* Newbury Park, CA: Sage.

Green, R. S., & Gracely, E. J. (1987). Selecting a rating scale for evaluating services to the chronically mentally ill. *Community Mental Health Journal, 23*, 91-102.

Grob, G. N. (1987). The forging of mental health policy in America: World War II to New Frontier. *Journal of the History of Medicine and Allied Sciences, 42*, 410-446.

Grove, W. M., Andreasen, N. C., McDonald-Scott, P., Keller, M. B., & Shapiro, R. W. (1981). Reliability studies of psychiatric diagnosis. *Archives of General Psychiatry, 38*, 408-416.

Gruenberg, A. M. (1986). An epidemiological perspective on mental disorder nosology. In A. M. Freedman, R. Brotman, I. Silverman, & D. Hutson (Eds.), *Issues in psychiatric classification* (pp. 142-149). New York: Human Sciences Press.

Gruenberg, A. M., Kendler, K. S., & Tsuang, M. T. (1985). Reliability and concordance in the subtyping of schizophrenia. *American Journal of Psychiatry, 142*, 1355-1358.

Gurland, B. J., & Cross, P. S. (1982). Epidemiology of psychopathology in old age: Some implications for clinical services. *Psychiatric Clinics of North America, 5*, 11-26.

Gurland, B. J., Mann, A., Cross, P. S., DeFiguerido, J., Shannon, M., Mann, A. H., Jenkins, R., Bennett, R., Wilder, D., Wright, H., Killeffer, E., Godlove, C., Thompson, P., Ross, M., & Deming, W. E. (1979). A cross national comparison of the institutionalized elderly in the cities of New York and London. *Psychological Medicine, 9*, 781-788.

Hamilton, M. (1982). Symptoms and assessment of depression. In E. S. Payket (Ed.), *Handbook of affective disorders* (pp. 3-11). New York: Guilford Press.

Hammersley, M., & Atkinson, P. (1983). *Ethnography: Principles in practice*. London: Tavistock.

Hansagi, H., Norell, S. E., & Magnusson, G. (1985). Hospital care utilization in a 17,000 population sample: 5-year follow-up. *Social Science and Medicine, 20*, 487-492.

Hart, K. (1989). Is academic freedom bad for business? *Bulletin of the Atomic Scientists, 45*(3), 28-34.

Haviland, M. G., Pincus, H. A., & Dial, T. H. (1987). Career, research involvement, and research fellowship plans of potential psychiatrists. *Archives of General Psychiatry, 44*, 493-496.

Hays, J. R. (1975). The ethics of unobtrusive research. In J. C. Schoolar & C. M. Gaitz (Eds.), *Research and the psychiatric patient* (pp. 165-174). New York: Brunner/Mazel.

Helzer, J. E., Robins, L. N., Croughan, J. L., & Welner, A. (1981). Renard Diagnostic Interview: Its reliability and procedural validity with physicians and lay interviewers. *Archives of General Psychiatry, 38*, 393-398.

Helzer, J. E., Spitznagel, E. L., & McEvoy, L. (1987). The predictive validity of lay Diagnostic Interview Schedule diagnoses in the general population: A comparison with physician examiners. *Archives of General Psychiatry, 44*, 1069-1077.

Hendrickson, L., & Myers, J. (1973). Some sources and potential consequences of errors in medical data recording. *Methods of Information Medicine, 12*, 38-45.

Hickey, J. S., & Baer, P. E. (1988). Psychological approaches to the assessment and treatment of anxiety and depression. *Medical Clinics of North America, 72*, 911-927.

Hogarty, G. E., Goldberg, S. C., Schooler, N. R., Ulrich, R. F., the Collaborative Study Group. (1974). Drug and sociotherapy in the aftercare of schizophrenic patients. *Archives of General Psychiatry, 31*, 603-608.

Hollingshead, A. B., & Redlich, F. C. (1958). *Social class and mental illness: A community study*. New York: John Wiley.

Holmes, T. H., & Rahe, R. H. (1967). The social readjustment rating scale. *Journal of Psychosomatic Research, 11*, 213-225.

Holzer, C. E., Tischler, G. L., Leaf, P. J., & Myers, J. K. (1984). An epidemiological assessment of cognitive impairment in a community population. In J. R. Greenley (Ed.), *Research in community and mental health* (vol. 4, pp. 3-32). Greenwich, CT: JAI Press.

Hospital and Community Psychiatry. (1988). New rules exclude mentally ill retarded from nursing homes. *Hospital and Community Psychiatry, 39*, 452-453.

House, W. C., Miller, S. I., & Schlachter, R. H. (1978). Role definitions among mental health professionals. *Comprehensive Psychiatry, 19*, 469-476.

Hsiao, J. K., Bartko, J. J., & Potter, W. Z. (1989). Diagnosing diagnoses: Receiver operating characteristic methods and psychiatry. *Archives of General Psychiatry, 46*, 664-667.

Huber, G., Gross, G., Schuttler, R., & Linz, M. (1980). Longitudinal studies of schizophrenic patients. *Schizophrenia Bulletin, 6*, 592-604.

Hudson, B. L. (1982). *Social work with psychiatric patients*. London: MacMillan.

Hyman, H. (1954). *Interviewing in social research*. Chicago: University of Chicago Press.

Institute of Medicine. (1980). *Reliability of national hospital discharge survey data*. Washington, DC: National Academy of Sciences.

Irwin, M., Lovitz, A., Marder, S. R., Mintz, J., Winslade, W. J., VanPutten, T., & Mills, M. J. (1985). Psychotic patients' understanding of informed consent. *American Journal of Psychiatry, 142*, 1351-1354.

Johnstone, E. C. (1986). Schizophrenia: Measurement and assessment. In G. D. Burrows, T. R. Norman, & G. Rubinstein (Eds.), *Handbook of studies on schizophrenia, part I* (pp. 159-168). New York: Elsevier Science.

Jorgensen, D. (1989). *Participant observation: A methodology for human studies*. Newbury Park, CA: Sage.

Junker, B. (1960). *Field work*. Chicago: University of Chicago Press.

Kaplan, H. I., & Sadock, B. J. (1989). *Comprehensive textbook of psychiatry/V* (Vol. 1 & 2). Baltimore, MD: Williams & Wilkins.

Katz, M. M., & Lyerly, S. (1963). Methods for measuring adjustment and social behavior in the community: I—Rationale, description, discriminative validity and scale development. *Psychological Reports, 13*, 503-535.

Keith, S. J., & Matthews, S. (Eds.). (1988). *A national plan for research on schizophrenia* (DHHS publication No. ADM 88-1571). Washington, DC: Government Printing Office.

Keith, S. J., Sirovatka, P., Matthews, S., & Corbett, M. (1987). A national plan for research on schizophrenia: Background and overview (draft). Rockville, MD: National Institutes of Mental Health.

Kellam, S. G., Schmelzer, J. L., & Berman, A. (1966). Variation in the atmospheres of psychiatric wards. *Archives of General Psychiatry, 14*, 561-570.

Kelly, G. R., Mamon, J. A., & Scott, J. E. (1987). Utility of the health belief model in examining medication compliance among psychiatric outpatients. *Social Science and Medicine, 25*, 1205-1211.

Kendell, R. E. (1986). What are mental disorders. In A. M. Freedman, R. Brotman, I. Silverman, & D. Hutson (Eds.), *Issues in psychiatric classification* (pp. 23-45). New York: Human Sciences Press.

Keyser, D. J., & Sweetland, R. C. (Eds.). (1985). *Test critiques*. Kansas City, MO: Test Corporation of America.

Kiesler, C. A., Simpkins, C., & Morton, T. (1990). Predicting length of hospital stay for psychiatric inpatients. *Hospital and Community Psychiatry, 41*, 149-154.

Kingsbury, S. J. (1987). Cognitive difference between clinical psychologists and psychiatrists. *American Psychologist, 42*, 152-156.

Kirscht, J. P. (1988). The health belief model and predictions of health actions. In D. S. Gochman (Ed.), *Health behavior: Emerging research perspectives* (pp. 27-39). New York: Plenum.

Klerman, G. L. (1985). Diagnosis of psychiatric disorders in epidemiologic field studies. *Archives of General Psychiatry, 42*, 723-724.

Klerman, G. L. (1989). Comment on "Psychiatric diagnosis as reified measurement." *Journal of Health and Social Behavior, 30*, 26-34.

Koran, L. M. (1975). The reliability of clinical methods, data and judgments. *New England Journal of Medicine, 293*, 695-701.

Kraemer, H. C., Pruyn, J. P., Gibbons, R. D., Greenshouse, J. B., Grochocinski, V. J., Waternaux, C., & Kupfer, D. J. (1987). Methodology in psychiatric research: Report on the 1986 MacArthur Foundation Network I Methodology Institute. *Archives of General Psychiatry, 44*, 1100-1106.

Krakowski, M., Volavka, J., & Brizer, D. (1986). Psychopathology and violence: A review of the literature. *Comprehensive Psychiatry, 27*, 131-148.

Kreisman, D. E., & Joy, V. D. (1975). The family as reactor to the mental illness of a relative. In M. Guttentag & E. L. Struening (Eds.), *Handbook of evaluation research* (Vol. 2, pp. 483-518). Beverly Hills, CA: Sage.

Kupfer, D. (1976). REM latency—A psychobiological marker for primary depressive disease. *Biological Psychiatry, 2*, 159-174.

Langner, T. S. (1962). A twenty-two item screening score of psychiatric symptoms indicating impairment. *Journal of Health and Social Behavior, 3*, 269-276.

Laska, E. (1981). Developments in computerization of the psychiatric record. In C. Siegel & S. K. Fischer (Eds.), *Psychiatric records in mental health care* (pp. 271-296). New York: Brunner/Mazel.

Leaf, R. J. (1986). Mental health systems research: Adequacy of available organizational and systems data. In W. R. Scott & B. L. Black (Eds.), *The organization of mental health services: Societal and community systems* (pp. 97-129). Beverly Hills, CA: Sage.

Lehman, A. F. (1987). Capitation payment and mental health care: A review of the opportunities and risks. *Hospital and Community Psychiatry, 38*, 31-38.

Lehman, A. F., Myers, C. P., & Corty, E. (1989). Assessment and classification of patients with psychiatric and substance abuse syndromes. *Hospital and Community Psychiatry, 40*, 1019-1030.

Lemert, E. M. (1951). *Social pathology*. New York: McGraw-Hill.

Lewis, P., Rack, P. H., Vaddadi, K. S., & Allen, J. J. (1980). Ethnic differences in drug response. *Postgraduate Medical Journal 56*, 46-49.

Liberman, R. P., Falloon, I. R. H., & Wallace, C. J. (1984). Drug-psychosocial interactions in the treatment of schizophrenia. In M. Mirabi (Ed.), *The chronically mentally ill: Research and services* (pp. 175-212). New York: Spectrum.

Lidtz, T. (1963). *The family and human adaptation*. New York: International Universities Press.

Lidz, C. W., Meisel, A., Zerubavel, E., Carter, M., Sestak, R. M., & Roth, L. H. (1984). *Informed consent: A study of decision making in psychiatry*. New York: Guilford Press.

Lilienfeld, A. M., & Lilienfeld, D. E. (1980). *Foundations of epidemiology* (2nd ed.). New York: Oxford University Press.

Link, B. G., & Cullen, F. (1986). Contact with the mentally ill and perceptions of how dangerous they are. *Journal of Health and Social Behavior, 27*, 289-302.

Link, B. G., Dohrenwend, B. P., & Skiodol, A. E. (1986). Socio-economic status and schizophrenia: Noisome occupational characteristics as a risk factor. *American Sociological Review, 51*, 242-258.

Lion, J. R., Snyder, W., & Merrill, G. L. (1981). Underreporting of assaults on staff in a state hospital. *Hospital and Community Psychiatry, 32*, 497-498.

Lipsey, M. (1990). *Design sensitivity: Statistical power for experimental research.* Newbury Park, CA: Sage.

Marcus, L., Plasky, P., & Salzman, C. (1988). Effects of psychotropic drugs on memory: Part I. *Hospital and Community Psychiatry, 39*, 255-256.

Martin, R. L., & Preskorn, S. H. (1986). Use of the laboratory in psychiatry. In G. Winokur & P. Clayton (Eds.), *The medical basis of psychiatry* (pp. 522-540). Philadelphia: W. B. Saunders.

Mazure, C., Nelson, J. C., & Price, L. H. (1986). Reliability and validity of the symptoms of major depressive illness. *Archives of General psychiatry, 43*, 451-457.

McArthur, J. C. (1987). Updates on HIV infection: Neurological aspects. *Maryland Medical Journal, 36*, 32-34.

McEvoy, J. P., Hatcher, A., Appelbaum, P. S., & Abernethy, V. (1983). Chronic schizophrenic women's attitudes towards sex, pregnancy, birth control, and childbearing. *Hospital and Community Psychiatry, 34*, 536-539.

McGlashan, T. H. (1989). Schizophrenia: Psychodynamic theories. In H. I. Kaplan & B. J. Sadock (Eds.), *Comprehensive textbook of psychiatry/V* (Vol. 1) (pp. 745-756). Baltimore, MD: Williams & Wilkins.

Mechanic, D. (1969). *Mental health and social policy.* Englewood Cliffs, NJ: Prentice-Hall.

Mendlewicz, J., Fleiss, J. L., Cataldo, M., & Rainer, J. D. (1975). Accuracy of the family history method in affective illness: Comparison with direct interviews in family studies. *Archives of General Psychiatry, 32*, 309-314.

Mezochow, J., Miller, S., Seixas, F., & Frances, R. J. (1987). The impact of cost containment on alcohol and drug treatment. *Hospital and Community Psychiatry, 38*, 506-510.

Miller, I. W., Bishop, S., Norman, W. H., & Maddever, H. (1985). The modified Hamilton Rating Scale for Depression: Reliability and validity. *Psychiatric Research, 14*, 131-142.

Miller, S. M. (1952). The participant observer and "over-rapport." *American Sociological Review, 17*, 97-99.

Mirowsky J., & Ross, C. E. (1989a). Psychiatric diagnosis as reified measurement. *Journal of Health and Social Behavior, 30*, 11-25.

Mirowsky, J., & Ross, C. E. (1989b). *Social causes of psychological distress.* New York: Aldine.

Moran, P. W., & Lambert, M. J. (1983). A review of current assessment tools for monitoring changes in depression. In M. J. Lambert, E. R. Christensen, & S. S. DeJulio, (Eds.), *The assessment of psychotherapy outcome* (pp. 263-303). New York: John Wiley.

Morgan, M., Calnan, M., & Manning, N. (1985). *Sociological approaches to health and medicine.* London: Croom Helm.

Mossman, D., & Somoza, E. (1989). Maximizing diagnostic information from the dexamethasone suppression test: Receiver operating characteristic analysis. *Archives of General Psychiatry, 46*, 653-663.

Mulford, H. A., & Miller, D. E. (1951). Drinking in Iowa 1. Socio-cultural distribution of drinkers: With a methodological model for sampling evaluation and interpretation of findings. *Quarterly Journal of Studies on Alcohol, 20*, 704-726.

Mulligan, M. J., Steer, R. A., & Fine, E. W. (1978). Psychiatric disturbances in drunk driving offenders referred for treatment of alcoholism. *Alcoholism, 2*, 107-111.

Murnaghan, J. H., & White, K. L. (1971). Hospital patient statistics: Problems and prospects. *New England Journal of Medicine, 284*, 822-828.

Myers, J., & Weissman, M. M. (1980). Use of a self-report symptom scale to detect depression in a community sample. *American Journal of Psychiatry, 137*, 1081-1084.

Myers, J. K., Weissman, M. M., Tischler, G. L., Holzer, C. E., Leaf, P. J., Orvaschel, H., Anthony, J. C., Boyd, J. H., Burke, J. D., Jr., Kramer, M., & Stoltzman, R. (1984). Six-month prevalence of psychiatric disorders in three communities: 1980 to 1982. *Archives of General Psychiatry, 41*, 959-967.

National Advisory Mental Health Council. (1989). *Approaching the 21st century: Opportunities for NIMH neuroscience research* (DHHS publication No. ADM 89-1580). Washington, DC: Government Printing Office.

National Commission for the Protection of Human Subjects of Biomedical and Behavioral Research. (1978). *Research involving those institutionalized as mentally infirm: Report and recommendations* (DHEW No. 78-0006). Washington, DC: Government Printing Office.

Navia, B. A., Price, R. W. (1987). The acquired immunodeficiency syndrome dementia complex as the presenting or sole manifestation of human immunodeficiency virus infection. *Archives of Neurology, 44*, 65-69.

Nelson, K. M. (1986). Economic considerations of diagnosis. In A. M. Freedman, R. Brotman, I. Silverman, & D. Hutson (Eds.), *Issues in psychiatric classification* (pp. 160-171). New York: Human Sciences Press.

Neuchterlien, K., & Dawson M. E. (1984). Vulnerability and stress factors in the developmental course of schizophrenic disorders. *Schizophrenia Bulletin, 10*, 158-312.

Neyman, J. (1955). Statistics—Servant of all sciences. *Science, 122*, 401.

Nunnally, J. C. (1978). *Psychometric theory* (2nd ed.). New York: McGraw-Hill.

Nurius, P. S., & Gibson, J. W. (1990). Clinical observation, inference, reasoning, and judgment in social work: An update. *Social Work Research and Abstracts, 26*, 18-25.

Overall, J. E., & Gorham, D. R. (1962). The brief psychiatric rating scale. *Psychological Reports, 10*, 799-812.

Parsons, T. (1951). *The social system.* New York: Free Press.

Parsons, T. (1975). The sick role and the role of the physician reconsidered. *Milbank Memorial Fund Quarterly, 53*, 257-277.

Paul, S. M. (1988). Anxiety and depression: A common neurobiological substrate? *Journal of Clinical Psychiatry, 49*(Supp.), 13-16.

Perlman, B. B., Schwartz, A. H., Paris, M., Thornton, J. C., Smith, H., & Weber, R. (1982). Psychiatric records: Variations based on discipline and patient characteristics, with implications for quality of care. *American Journal of Psychiatry 139*, 1154-1157.

Perrucci, R., & Targ, D. B. (1982). *Mental patients and social networks.* Boston: Auburn House.

Perry, S. W., & Markowitz, J. (1986). Psychiatric interventions for AIDS-spectrum disorders. *Hospital and Community Psychiatry, 37*, 1001-1006.

Pharis, D. B. (1989). State hospital reform in Texas: A history of the R.A.J. class action lawsuit. In C. M. Bonjean, M. T. Coleman, & I. Iscoe (Eds.), *Community care of the chronically mentally ill* (pp. 205-220). Austin: The University of Texas, The Hogg Foundation for Mental Health.

Pliszka, S. R. (1990). Recent child mental health research in Texas: A review. In C. M. Bonjean & D. J. Foss (Eds.), *Mental health research in Texas: Retrospect and prospect* (pp. 306-320). Austin: The University of Texas, The Hogg Foundation for Mental Health.

Popkin, M. K. (1986). Organic brain syndromes presenting with global cognitive impairment: Delirium and dementia. In G. Winokur & P. Clayton (Eds.), *The medical basis of psychiatry* (pp. 3-19). Philadelphia: W. B. Saunders.

Rabkin, J. G. (1980). Determinants of public attitudes about mental illness: Summary of the research literature. In J. G. Rabkin, L. Gelb, & J. B. Lazar (Eds.), *Attitudes toward the mentally ill: Research perspectives* (pp. 27-31). Washington, DC: National Institutes of Mental Health.

Radloff, L. S. (1977). The CES-D Scale: A self-report depression scale for research in the general population. *Applied Psychological Measurement, 1*, 385-401.

Rancurello, M. D. (1988). Research training in psychiatry: Considerations at the preresidency level. *Psychopharmacology Bulletin, 24*, 293-299.

Rappeport, J. R., Lassen, G., & Hay, N. B. (1967). A review of the literature on the dangerousness of the mentally ill. In J. R. Rappeport (Ed.), *The clinical evaluation of the dangerousness of the mentally ill*, (pp. 72-80). Springfield, IL: Charles C Thomas.

Regier, D. A., Myers, J. K., Kramer, M., Robins, L. N., Blazer, D. G., Hough, R. L., Eaton, W. W., & Locke, B. Z. (1984). The NIMH Epidemiologic Catchment Area program. *Archives of General Psychiatry, 41*, 934-941.

Reich, J., Black, D. W., & Jarjoua, D. (1987). Architecture of research in psychiatry, 1953-1983. *Archives of General Psychiatry, 44*, 311-313.

Research and Education Association. (1981). *Handbook of psychiatric scales*. New York: Author.

Rieder, R. O. (1988). The recruitment and training of psychiatric residents for research. *Psychopharmacology Bulletin, 24*, 288-290.

Ritter, C. (1988). Social supports, social networks and health behavior. In D. S. Gochman (Ed.), *Health behavior: Emerging research perspectives* (pp. 149-162). New York: Plenum.

Robins, L. (1983). Continuities and discontinuities in the psychiatric disorders of children. In D. Mechanic (Ed.), *Handbook of health, health care, and the health professions* (pp. 195-219). New York: Free Press.

Robins, L. (1989). DIS-III-R progress. *DIS Newsletter, 6*, 1.

Robins, L. N., Helzer, J. E., Croughan, J., & Ratcliff, K. S. (1981). National Institute of Mental Health Diagnostic Interview Schedule: Its history, characteristics, and validity. *Archives of General Psychiatry, 38*, 381-389.

Robins, L. N, Wing, J., Wittchen, H. U., Helzer, J. E., Babor, T. F., Burke, J., Farmer, A., Jablenski, A., Pickens, R., Regier, D. A., Sartorius, N., & Towle, L. H. (1988). The composite international diagnostic interview. *Archives of General Psychiatry, 45*, 1069-1077.

Roos, L. L., & Nicol, J. P. (1981). Research designs for data banks. *Evaluation Review, 5*, 501-523.

Roos, L. L., Roos, N. P., Cageorge, S. M., & Nicol, J. P. (1982). How good are the data? Reliability of one health care data bank. *Medical Care, 20*, 266-276.

Rosenbaum, C. P. (1970). *The meaning of madness: Symptomatology, sociology, biology, and therapy of the schizophrenias.* New York: Science House.

Rosenberg, M. (1984). A symbolic interactionist view of psychosis. *Journal of Health and Social Behavior, 25,* 289-302.

Rosenhan, D. L. (1973). On being sane in insane places. *Science, 179,* 250-258.

Rosenheck, R., & Astrachan, B. (1990). Regional variation in patterns of inpatient psychiatric care. *American Journal of Psychiatry, 147,* 1180-1183.

Rosenstock, I. M. (1966). Why people use health services. *Milbank Memorial Fund Quarterly, 44,* 94-127.

Rosoff, A. J. (1981). *Informed consent: A guide for health care providers.* Rockville, MD: Aspen Systems Corporation.

Ross, A. O. (1978). Behavior therapy with children. In S. L. Garfield & A. E. Pergin (Eds.), *Handbook of psychotherapy and behavior change: An empirical analysis* (2nd ed.). New York: John Wiley.

Ross, H. E., Glaser, F. B., & Germanson, T. (1988). The prevalence of psychiatric disorders in patients with alcohol and other drug problems. *Archives of General Psychiatry, 45,* 1023-1031.

Rossi, P. H., & Whyte, W. F. (1983). The applied side of sociology. In H. E. Freeman, R. R. Dynes, P. H. Rossi, & W. F. Whyte (Eds.), *Applied sociology* (pp. 5-31). San Francisco: Jossey-Bass.

Rossor, M. (1984). Biological markers in mental disorders: Post-mortem studies. *Journal of Psychiatric Research, 18,* 457-465.

Ruby, G. (1984). The policy implications of insurance coverage for psychiatric services. *International Journal of Law and Psychiatry, 7,* 269-284.

Rupp, A., Steinwachs, D. M., & Salkever, D. S. (1985). Hospital payment effects on acute inpatient care for mental disorders. *Archives of General Psychiatry, 42,* 552-555.

Rutter, M. (1986). Meyerian psychobiology, personality development, and the role of life experiences. *American Journal of Psychiatry, 143,* 1077-1087.

Salek, W. M. (1988). Use of a microcomputer relational database in a long-term-care psychiatric facility. *American Journal of Hospital Pharmacy, 45,* 1907-1908.

Salsburg, D. S. (1985). The religion of statistics as practiced in medical journals. *The American Statistician, 39,* 220-223.

Sappington, A. A., & Michaux, M. H. (1975). Prognostic patterns in self-report, relative report, and professional evaluation measures for hospitalized and day-care patients. *Journal of Consulting and Clinical Psychology, 43,* 904-910.

Scheff, T. J. (1966). *Being mentally ill: A sociological theory.* New York: Aldine.

Schless, A. P., & Mendels, J. (1978). The value of interviewing family and friends in assessing life stressors. *Archives of General Psychiatry, 35,* 565-567.

Schwab, J. J., & Schwab, M. E. (1978). *Sociocultural roots of mental illness: An epidemiologic survey.* New York: Plenum.

Schwartz, A. H., Perlman, B. B., Paris, M., Schmidt, K., & Thornton, J. C. (1980). Psychiatric diagnoses as reported to Medicaid and as recorded in patient charts. *American Journal of Public Health, 70,* 406-408.

Schwartz, J. E., Pieper, C. F., & Karasek, R. A. (1988). A procedure for linking psychosocial job characteristics data to health surveys. *American Journal of Public Health, 78,* 904-909.

Scott, W. R., & Black, B. L. (Eds.). (1986). *The organization of mental health services: Society and community systems.* Beverly Hills, CA: Sage.

Shapiro, L. J., Comings, D. E., Jones, O. W., & Rimoin, D. L. (1986). New frontiers in genetic medicine. *Annals of Internal Medicine, 104,* 527-539.

Sheehan, J. S. (1982). *Is there no place on earth for me?* New York: Random House.

Sieber, J. (1991). *Planning ethically responsible research: Developing an effective protocol.* Newbury Park, CA: Sage.

Siegel, C., & Fischer, S. K. (1981a). Development and present structure of the psychiatric record. In C. Siegel & S. K. Fischer (Eds.), *Psychiatric records in mental health care* (pp. 3-84). New York: Brunner/Mazel.

Siegel, C., & Fischer, S. K. (1981b). A national questionnaire survey of mental health professionals on their uses of and attitudes toward psychiatric records. In C. Siegel & S. K. Fischer (Eds.), *Psychiatric records in mental health care* (pp. 87-120). New York: Brunner/Mazel.

Siegel, C., & Fischer, S. K. (1981c). A field study of the clinical uses of psychiatric records. In C. Siegel & S. K. Fischer (Eds.), *Psychiatric records in mental health care* (pp. 121-204). New York: Brunner/Mazel.

Silverman, I. (1986). On the uses and misuses of psychiatric classification. In A. M. Freedman, R. Brotman, I. Silverman, & D. Hutson (Eds.), *Issues in psychiatric classification* (pp. 195-211). New York: Human Sciences Press.

Silverman, I., & Brotman, R. (1986). The issue of credibility in practice. In A. M. Freedman, R. Brotman, I. Silverman, & D. Hutson (Eds.), *Issues in psychiatric classification* (pp. 164-171). New York: Human Sciences Press.

Singer, E., Frankel, M. R., & Glassman, M. B. (1983). The effect of interviewer characteristics and expectation on response. *The Public Opinion Quarterly, 47,* 68-83.

Smith, J. O., Sjoberg, G., & Phillips, V. A. (1969). The use and meaning of psychiatric records: A research note. *International Journal of Social Psychiatry, 15,* 129-135.

Snow, D. A., Baker, S. G., & Anderson, L. (1988). On the precariousness of measuring insanity in insane contexts. *Social Problems, 35,* 192-196.

Snow, D. A., Baker, S. G., Anderson, L., & Martin, M. (1986). The myth of pervasive mental illness among the homeless. *Social Problems, 33,* 407-423.

Spiegel, R., & Aebi, H. J. (1981). *Psychopharmacology.* Chichester, UK: John Wiley.

Spitzer, R., & Endicott, J. (1971). An integrated group of forms for automated psychiatric case records. *Archives of General Psychiatry, 42,* 540-547.

Spitzer, R. L., Endicott, J., & Robins, E. (1975). Clinical criteria for psychiatric diagnosis and DSM-III. *American Journal of Psychiatry, 132,* 1187-1192.

Spitzer, R. L., & Williams, J. B. W. (1988). Revised diagnostic criteria and a new structured interview for diagnosing anxiety disorders. *Journal of Psychiatric Research, 22* (Supp. 1), 55-85.

Srole, L., Langner, T. S., Michael, S. T., Opler, M. K., & Rennie, T. A. C. (1962). *Mental health in the metropolis. The midtown Manhattan study.* New York: McGraw-Hill.

Stanton, A. H., & Schwartz, M. S. (1954). *The mental hospital.* New York: Basic Books.

Stephens, J. H., Astrup, C., Carpenter, W. T., Shaffer, J. W., & Goldberg, J. (1982). A comparison of nine systems to diagnose schizophrenia. *Psychiatry Research, 6,* 127-143.

Stevens, M., Crow, T. J., Bowman, M. J., & Coles, E. C. (1978). Age disorientation in chronic schizophrenia: A constant prevalence of 25% in a chronic mental hospital population. *British Journal of Psychiatry, 133,* 130-136.

Stimson, G., & Webb, B. (1989). Face-to-face interaction. In P. Brown (Ed.), *Perspectives in medical sociology* (pp. 519-529). Belmont, CA: Wadsworth.

Stokes, P. E. (1988). Bipolar disorders. In J. J. Mann (Ed.), *Phenomenology of depressive illness* (pp. 97-125). New York: Human Sciences Press.

Strayhorn, J. M. (1987). Control groups for psychosocial intervention outcome studies. *American Journal of Psychiatry, 144*, 275-282.

Stromgren, E. (1986). The rise and fall of the concept "first admission." *American Journal of Social Psychiatry, 6*, 227-229.

Strupp, H. H., & Hadley, S. W. (1977). A tripartite model of mental health and therapeutic outcomes with special reference to negative effects in psychotherapy. *American Psychologist, 32*, 187-196.

Szasz, T. S. (1961). *The myth of mental illness.* New York: Hoeber- Harper.

Targum, S. D., Dibble, E. D., Davenport, Y. B., & Gershon, E. S. (1981). The Family Attitudes Questionnaire: Patients' and spouses' views of bipolar illness. *Archives of General Psychiatry,38*, 562-568.

Taub, H. A. (1986). Comprehension of informed consent for research: Issues and directions for future study. *IRB: A Review of Human Subjects Research, 8*, 7-10.

Taylor, P. J. (1986). The risk of violence in psychotics. *Integrative Psychiatry, 4*, 12-24.

Teplin, L. A. (1990). The prevalence of severe mental disorder among male urban jail detainees: Comparison with the Epidemiologic Catchment Area Program. *American Journal of Public Health, 80*, 663-669.

Tessler, R. C., & Dennis, D. L. (1989). A synthesis of NIMH-funded research concerning persons who are homeless and mentally ill. Rockville, MD: National Institutes of Mental Health.

Thompson, W. D., Orvaschel, H., Prusoff, B. A., & Kidd, K. K. (1982). An evaluation of the family history method for ascertaining psychiatric disorders. *Archives of General Psychiatry, 39*, 53-58.

Tomlinson, B. E. (1980). The structural and quantitative aspects of the dementias. In P. J. Roberts (Ed.), *The biochemistry of dementia* (pp. 5-52). Chichester, UK: John Wiley.

Torrey, E. F. (1988). *Surviving schizophrenia: A family manual.* New York: Harper & Row.

Tsuang, M. T., & Loyd, D. W. (1986). Schizophrenia. In G. Winokur, & P. Clayton (Eds.), *The medical basis of psychiatry* (pp. 80-101). Philadelphia: W. B. Saunders.

Tsuang, M. T., & Winokur, G. (1974). Criteria for subtyping schizophrenia: Clinical differentiation of hebephrenic and paranoid schizophrenia. *Archives of General Psychiatry, 31*, 43-47.

Twaddle, A. C. (1979). *Sickness behavior and the sick role.* Boston: G. K. Hall.

Tweed, D. L., & George, L. K. (1989). Comment on "Psychiatric diagnosis as reified measurement." *Journal of Health and Social Behavior, 30*, 35-38.

U. S. Department of Health and Human Services. (1980). *The international classification of diseases, 9th revision: Clinical modification, vols. 1-3* (DHHS Publication No. PHS 80-1260). Washington, DC: Government Printing Office.

Vaillant, G. E., Schnurr, P. (1988). What is a case? *Archives of General Psychiatry, 45*, 313-319.

Vernon, S. A., & Roberts, R. E. (1982). Use of the SADS-RDC in a tri-ethnic community survey. *Archives of General Psychiatry, 39*, 47-52.

Vestre, N. D., & Zimmermann, R. (1969). Validity of informants' ratings of the behavior and symptoms of psychiatric patients. *Journal of Consulting and Clinical Psychology, 33*, 175-179.

Vidich, A. J. (1955). Participant observation and the collection and interpretation of data. *American Journal of Sociology, 60*, 354-360.

Wallston, B. S., Wallston, K. A., Kaplan, G. D., & Maides, S. A. (1976). Development and validation of the Health Locus of Control (MHLC) Scale. *Journal of Consulting and Clinical Psychology, 44*, 580-585.

Wallston, K. A., & Wallston, B. S. (1982). Who is responsible for your health? The construct of health locus of control. In G. S. Sanders & J. Suls (Eds.), *Social psychology of health and illness* (pp. 65-95). Hillsdale, NJ: Lawrence Erlbaum.

Warner, R. (1985). *Recovery from schizophrenia: Psychiatry and political economy.* London: Routledge & Kegan Paul.

Warren, J. W., Sobal, J., Tenney, J. H., Hoopes, J. M., Damron, D., Levenson, S., DeForge, B. R., & Muncie, H. L., Jr. (1986). Informed consent by proxy: An issue in research with elderly patients. *New England Journal of Medicine, 315*, 1124-1128.

Waters, K. A., & Murphy, G. F. (1979). *Medical records in health information.* Germantown, MD: Aspen Systems Corporation.

Webb, E. J., Campbell, D. T., Schwartz, R. D., & Sechrest, L. (1966). *Unobtrusive measures: Nonreactive research in the social sciences.* Chicago: Rand McNally.

Weed, L. L. (1971). *Medical records, medical evaluation, and patient care.* Cleveland, OH: Press of Case Western Reserve University.

Weiss, C. H. (1972). *Evaluation research: Methods of assessing program effectiveness.* Englewood Cliffs, NJ: Prentice-Hall.

Weiss, C. H. (1975). Interviewing in evaluation research. In E. L. Struening & M. Guttentag (Eds.), *Handbook of evaluation research* (Vol. 1, pp. 355-395). Beverly Hills, CA: Sage.

Weiss, S. H., & Biggar, R. J. (1986). The epidemiology of human retrovirus-associated illness. *Mount Sinai Journal of Medicine, 53*, 579-590.

Weissman, M. M., & Bothwell, S. (1976). Assessment of social adjustment by patient self-report. *Archives of General Psychiatry, 33*, 1111-1115.

Weissman, M. M., Leaf, P. J., Tischler, G. L., Blazer, D. G., Karno, M., Bruce, M. L., & Florio, L. P. (1988). Affective disorders in five United States communities. *Psychological Medicine, 18*, 141-153.

Weissman, M. M., & Myers, J. K. (1978). Affective disorders in a United States urban community: The use of Research Diagnostic Criteria in an epidemiological survey. *Archives of General Psychiatry, 35*, 1304-1311.

Weissman, M. M., Myers, J. K., & Ross, C. E. (Eds.). (1986a). *Community surveys of psychiatric disorders.* New Brunswick, NJ: Rutgers University Press.

Weissman, M. M., Myers, J. K., & Ross, C. E. (1986b). Community studies in psychiatric epidemiology: An introduction. In M. M. Weissman, J. K. Myers, & C. E. Ross (Eds.), *Community surveys of psychiatric disorders* (pp. 1-19). New Brunswick, NJ: Rutgers University Press.

Wells, K. B., Burnam, M. A., Leake, B., & Robins, L. N. (1988). Agreement between face-to-face and telephone-administered versions of the depression section of the NIMH Diagnostic Interview Schedule. *Journal of Psychiatric Research, 22*, 207-220.

West, C. (1989). Talcott Parson's "sick role" and its critiques. In P. Brown (Ed.), *Perspectives in medical sociology* (pp. 145-152). Belmont CA: Wadsworth.

Windle, C. (1980). Correlates of community mental health center underservice to non-whites. *Journal of Community Psychology, 8*, 140-146.

Wing, J. (1962). Institutionalism in mental hospitals. *British Journal of Psychiatry, 1*, 38-51.

Wing, J. K., Cooper, J. E., & Sartorius, N. (1974). *Measurement and classification of psychiatric symptoms: An instruction manual for the PSE and CATEGO program.* London: Cambridge University Press.

Wing, J. K., Mann, S. A., Leff, J. P., & Nixon, J. M. (1978) The concept of a "case" in psychiatric population surveys. *Psychological Medicine, 8,* 203-217.

Winokur, G. (1986). Unipolar depression. In G. Winokur & P. Clayton (Eds.), *The medical basis of psychiatry* (pp. 60-79). Philadelphia: W. B. Saunders.

Winokur, G., & Clayton, P. (Eds.). (1986). *The medical basis of psychiatry.* Philadelphia: W. B. Saunders.

Winokur, G., Zimmerman, M., & Cadoret, R. (1988). 'Cause the Bible tells me so. *Archives of General Psychiatry, 45,* 683-684.

Woolf, P. K. (1987). Ensuring integrity in biomedical publication. *Journal of the American Medical Association, 258,* 3424-3427.

Wright, J. D. (1988). The mentally ill homeless: What is myth and what is fact? *Social Problems, 35,* 182-191.

Yager, J., Grant, I., Sweetwood, H. L., & Gerst, M. (1981). Life event reports by psychiatric patients, nonpatients, and their partners. *Archives of General Psychiatry, 38,* 343-347.

Yahr, M. D., & Duvoisin, R. C. (1968). Medical therapy of Parkinsonism. *Medical Therapeutics, 5,* 283-300.

Young, C. L. (1986). Social work roles in collaborative research. *Social Work in Health Care, 11,* 71-81.

Zubin, J., Magazine, J., & Steinhauer, S. (1983). The metamorphosis of schizophrenia: From chronicity to vulnerability. *Psychological Medicine, 13,* 551-571.

Zung, W. W. K. (1965). A self-rating depression scale. *Archives of General Psychiatry, 12,* 65-70.

Index

About the Author

Rosalind J. Dworkin received her Ph.D. in Sociology from Northwestern University in 1974. Since then, she has worked in both traditional academic environments and in applied settings. She has worked in several areas of medical sociology, including abortion behavior, cardiovascular risk reduction, and adjustment to cancer. She has spent more than 7 years doing methodological and applied research on the chronically mentally ill and has published extensively in that area. She is currently an adjunct full professor at the University of Houston, and she is on the research staff of The Institute of Child and Family Services, an affiliate of DePelchin Children's Center in Houston, Texas.